D1524064

James Dickey

The Critic as Poet

James Dickey
The Critic as Poet

An Annotated Bibliography
With
An Introductory Essay

by

Eileen Glancy

The Whitston Publishing Company
Incorporated
Troy, New York
1971

PREFACE

Compiling a bibliography of works by and about James Dickey is a difficult project, for it is like aiming at a moving target. Mr. Dickey has written thirteen books in the past eleven years; another, a book of essays, is scheduled for publication before the end of this year (1971). A movie based on his novel, *Deliverance*, will be released this fall. Meanwhile, Mr. Dickey continues to publish poetry, and the critics persist in writing about him.

When an unannotated version of this bibliography appeared in *Twentieth Century Literature* in 1969, I commented that the indexes of periodical literature were quite inadequate in their listings on Dickey; unfortunately the situation has not changed in the past two years. I hope this checklist will make the material more accessible. My thanks are due to Mr. Dickey who so kindly invited me to his home to peruse his scrapbooks; and to Professor Jackson R. Bryer for his advice. I must take responsibility for any gaps or errors in the bibliography.

Eileen Glancy

INTRODUCTORY ESSAY

James Dickey published his first collection of poetry in 1960, and in a meteoric ten years he has published four additional books of poetry, two volumes of criticism and a novel. His achievement has been recognized by a wide audience: his novel is listed as a best seller, his poetry is discussed in the classroom, and his criticism is lauded by the critics. While *Deliverance* and *Poems 1957–1967* have received the most attention, the praise for *Babel to Byzantium* might be the most important indication of Dickey's accomplishment. The astute critic Ralph J. Mills, Jr., writes, "James Dickey's critical book is the most perceptive one we have had on contemporary poetry since Randall Jarrell's *Poetry and The Age* appeared well over a decade ago." Mills and others, who have recently recognized Dickey as a critic, have placed him in the tradition of T. S. Eliot and Randall Jarrell, poet-critics who influenced English poetry through their critical evaluations as well as through their creative efforts. This recognition and the suggestion that Dickey is following Jarrell as the poet-critic of our decade indicate the need for an examination of the poetic tenets of James Dickey. Moreover, the examples of the great poet-critics of English literature reveal the writer not only elucidating the poetry under consideration but also providing insights into his own poetry. Accordingly, Dickey's criticism should reveal poetic tenets which serve as a guide to his poetry. The purpose of this paper is to discover in Dickey's critical writings those standards by which he judges and to apply his criteria to his own poetry--to find if the poet preaches what he practices.

Although in his preface to *Babel to Byzantium* Dickey disclaims any "system of evaluation," especially the "full scale critical performance, the huge exegetical tome that quite literally uses up the creative work it purports to discuss," and "systems of ranking poets and poems," Dickey does have norms against which he consistently measures poetry. For example: does the poem have a particular vision or passion or a new perception? does the poem take the reader into the "opening world, to move among the vital potentialities of life and proclaim them?"

Dickey expressed one of his foremost tenets at a lecture at the Library of Congress; it is that poetry must go back "toward some basic things, ... to get back to wholeness of being, to respond fullheartedly and fullbodiedly to experience..." In an interview with Carolyn Kizer published in *Shenandoah*, Dickey explains that poetry is a corporeal experience for him: "There's not a lot of difference to me between playing a guitar and shooting a bow or writing a poem--just a difference of technique. It's a feeling of satisfaction from all three equally--and they complement each other," In the preface to *Babel to Byzantium*, Dickey suggests that he reads poetry in the same spirit: "...where poetry is concerned, there are more important things than judgment involved, and ... foremost among these is participation." Dickey is never detached; as a poet or critic he wants a poem to be experience. In the *Shenandoah* interview Dickey elaborated on his approach to life as well as art by quoting Henry James: "...'accessibility to experience': to go toward it, hoping it's going to be good or great. The psychological state with which one greets what comes to one is of absolute importance. ...I'll tell you what I dislike so much: ...the idea that everything is in some way sort of contemptible." In looking at the biography of the man, one could find the key words to be action, participation and perhaps "accessibility to experience."

At a poetry reading at the Library of Congress in 1968, James Dickey described his birthplace as "forty miles from Dalhonega, Georgia, chenille capital of the world," So much does he relish the South of rural, unsophisticated outdoorsmen that Dickey disguises his birthplace of Atlanta as the red hills of north Georgia. However unpoetic it may be, the poet was born in the South's largest city, where his father worked as a lawyer, and where he lived throughout his high school years. Dickey speaks of his attitude toward poetry during those years in "The Poet Turns on Himself":

> When I was in high school thirty years ago,
> I had courses in literature and memorized
> a number of poems, parts of which I can
> still remember, although I seldom do. From
> the class in poetry I went to another class
> in the basement of the school, which was
> called Manual Training and purported to
> to teach us how to work wood lathes, do a
> little light carpentry, weld, pour metals,
> and perform other similar tasks which I
> have not had occasion to repeat since that
> time. Then, however, I could not help
> being struck by the contrast between what
> we had been doing in the poetry class and
> the materials and skills--the means and
> the tangible results--of our work in Manual
> Training and, like every other American
> boy, I developed a strong bias in favor of
> learning how to *do* something, of being able

> to make something, of having at least in
> some degree a skill that paid off in "meas-
> urable entities." ...Yet even in my high
> school days I also began to be aware of a
> connection--a very disturbing and appar-
> ently necessary one--between words in a
> certain order and the events of my own life.

It is still the relationship of "words in a certain order and
events" rather than a fascination with words that is impor-
tant to Dickey.

After one year at Clemson College where he excelled
at the wonderfully measurable entities of football and track,
Dickey became a fighter pilot in World War II. It was during
this time that he became interested in writing and began
to search for "the right correlation between lived time--
experience--and words," but he admits "it was only years
later that I recognized that this quality I was seeking more
and more was poetry." Meanwhile as a pilot in the Pacific
Theater, Dickey completed eighty-seven missions and was
awarded a Silver Star and two Distinguished Flying Cross-
es. In 1946 Dickey enrolled in Vanderbilt University where
he was graduated in 1948 Magna Cum Laude, Phi Beta
Kappa and as a sprinting champion of Tennessee. In 1950
he received an M.A. degree from Vanderbilt. In the next
ten years the poet completed another tour of air duty in
Korea, taught at Rice Institute and the University of Flor-
ida and worked as an advertising copywriter. Not until
1961 after the publication of his first book, did Dickey
leave his successful business career and devote himself
completely to poetry; since that time he has served as
writer-in-residence at several universities and as Poetry
Consultant at the Library of Congress for two years, 1966--
1968. At present Dickey is a professor at the University

4

of South Carolina and serves as poetry editor for Esquire Magazine.

In his first book of criticism, *The Suspect in Poetry*, Dickey's thesis is that poetry is either suspect or genuine according to its relationship with reality. He acknowledges that "what may be suspect to me may well be genuine to you" and argues that that is not important: "What matters is that there be some real response to poems, some passionate and private feeling about them: that for certain people there be certain poems that speak directly to them as they believe God would." Dickey is suspicious of poems which rely on linguistic resourcefulness or "the bag of monkey-tricks of English poetry" rather than on an individual's imagination and vision. He blames the influence of Wallace Stevens, "whose mannered artificiality and poetry-about-writing-poetry-about-poetry have driven large numbers of writers delightedly back into their shimmering, wordy sensibilities and buried them there," for a situation in which "writing a poem is simply inventing a complex proposition about life or one of its manifestations, and illustrating it with what ever material appears to fit in." This approach results in a "particularly debilitated kind of puzzle-making sterility, where to over-complicate and then resolve is considered the criterion of artistic excellance." For Dickey, poetry intensifies life; it is not a superior amusement.

Because he wants a poem to have the direct impact of experience, Dickey is especially harsh with the timid poem dependent on literary rules and traditions, and with the poet who writes "into a Climate of poetic officialdom, or pretested Approval, based largely on the principles which the new Criticism has espoused, and on the opinions of those who Count in modern letters." For instance in

5

his review of Donald F. Drummond's *The Battlement*, Dickey writes:

> In common with almost all other Winters-trained writers, Drummond appears to have assimilated entirely, and to have put to extremely effective use, the well-known principles and techniques upon which Winters insists with his characteristic air of finality. This enables Drummond to operate with a certain measure of success within disastrously narrow bounds, and cuts him off entirely from writing poems of permanent value. Worse; one often has the feeling that Mr. Drummond is not a poet at all in the Platonic sense but is by choice a kind of minor artisan in words, who has learned all he can from his guild-master, and is unwilling or unable to contribute anything of his own.

The "minor artisan" errs by putting form above content, metre over metre making argument instead of finding his own form in his quest for a unique poetic voice.

In his emphasis on a personal vision and passion, Dickey does not neglect to chastise the poets who have no respect for tradition. Allen Ginsberg he pronounces the "perfect inhabitant if not the very founder of Babel"; his poetry is a "strewn, mishmash prose consisting mainly of assertion that its author is possessed...." Charles Olson and the projectivists, Dickey writes, suffer from "creative irresponsibility with a semblance of a rationale which may be defended in heated and cloudy terms by its supposed practitioners."

However, Dickey's most severe comments are not

aimed at expansive poems but at the overmannered and uninteresting, the over-intellectualized and unnecessary poems. Hayden Carruth's *The Crow and The Heart* is in this first category: "He seldom lets you forget that you are reading something which has been written, and written again, and then written some more." Dickey illustrates with a poem in which Carruth writes of a snowfall: "it is a decorator's description, with a great deal more emphasis on the describing than on the snow, and so we get a little shimmer of words and no sense of winter at all." A genuine poet's concern should be with the experience, "the sense of winter," not the words. At one point Dickey calls the poetry, "Carruth's verses-by-anybody" because they have the mechanical proficiency of a thousand versifiers and none of the particularity of a good poet. Dickey contends that it "is the compulsion to write one way rather than another, to say what one has to say in one way rather than another, the personal necessity for it, that makes good poets." Therefore, Dickey does not find Carruth's next book, *Journey to a Known Place*, overmannered or uninteresting: because "Mr. Carruth's Known Place is the world itself, seen and experienced, in and through its classic elements...."

The work of Thom Gunn, the highly esteemed English poet, falls into the over-intellectualized and unnecessary category. Dickey objects that the poetry "has not the slightest power to touch you...or to make you feel that the situation with which it is dealing has any importance whatever, except as material for the kind of poems Gunn writes." Dickey quotes from a poem about motorcyclists and questions Gunn's treatment of his material: "Isn't it a little silly to characterize a group of sideburned toughs on Harley-Davidsons as 'the self-defined, astride the cre-

ated will?' '' Dickey frets with the references Gunn makes
to birds and saints and towns where neither live and con-
cludes that they are irrelevant to the subject of the poem.
The fault here is that the poet is primarily concerned with
abstractions; the motorcyclists, birds and saints are sec-
ondary. Gunn's intellectual approach to poetry, his pose
of "universal wise man" has set him "increasingly far
from his subjects.''

     Dickey's approach to poetry is of course exactly op-
posite to Gunn's. Dickey admires a poem which begins
by waking the reader to the **potentiality** of everyday ex-
perience so that "the great simplicities, the illuminations...
come like the sun from behind the cloud of ordinary per-
ception and everyday judgments...." It is the poet's unique
vision and perception that enables him to elevate and clarify
experience. Because he stresses the value of the poet's
individuality, Dickey could say with Emerson, "Insist on
yourself.'' In his comments on E. E Cummings and Richard
Eberhart this is seen most explicitly. E. E. Cummings,
with the "superb arrogance of genius,'' is praised as a
"daringly original poet with more virility and more sheer,
uncompromising talent than any other living American writer'';
in the next breath Cummings is reprimanded for diluting
even the finest of his work with writing that is hardly more
than the "defiant playing of a child.'' The "arrogance of
genius'' and the "defiant playing'' are two sides of the
coin, and Dickey believes that the artist must cultivate
both.

> Just this jealous treasuring of his individ-
> uality, his uniqueness, has enabled Cum-
> mings' personality to flower in a number
> of perfectly inimitable poems,... beside
> which the efforts of all but a few other con-

temporary poets pale into competent indif-
ference....The important thing, however, is
that Cummings has felt the need, and fol-
lowed it, of developing absolutely in his
own way, of keeping himself and his writing
whole, preferring to harbor his most grevious
and obvious faults quite as if they were
part and parcel of his most original and val-
uable impulses, which perhaps they are.

Richard Eberhart's poetry is criticized in the same vein.
While objecting to the poet's "irritating mannerisms" and
"frivolous wordplay," Dickey praises his "conviction and
directness" with the conclusion: "I don't know whether or
not this kind of clairvoyant simplicity would be available
to Eberhart if it were not for the unnatural and frequently
ludicrous excesses of the other poems." Dickey would
rather see a poet follow his own idiosyncrasies than an-
other's dictates.

When Dickey praises a favorite poet it is "because of
the way he sees and feels the aspects of life which are
compelling to him" and because of his ability to relate the
reader to a larger, more expansive view of life. Theodore
Roethke, whom Dickey calls the "finest poet now writing
in English," is placed in the "company of the great Em-
pathizers, like Rilke and D. H. Lawrence....They are the
Awakeners, and can change your life not by telling but by
showing, not from the outside but from within, by lively
and persistently mysterious means of inducing you to be-
lieve that you were meant to perceive and know things as
Rilke, as Lawrence, as Roethke present them." Roethke
is commended for his "marvelous sensuous apprehension
of the natural world...and his total commitment to both
his vision and to the backbreaking craft of verse...."

Many critics have noticed the resemblance in mood and aspiration between Roethke and Dickey; if James Dickey has a mentor it must be Roethke. Dickey's comments on Roethke's poetry could be applied to Dickey's own:

> ...there is some mindless, elemental qual-
> ity in the sound of his voice, something
> primitive and animistic, something with the
> wariness and inhuman grace of the wild
> beast, and with it another thing that could
> not be and never has been animal-like.
> His poems are human poems in the full
> weight of that adjective: poems of a creature
> animal enough to enter half into unthinking
> nature and unanimal enough to be uneasy
> there, taking thought at what the animal
> half discerns and feels. This position,
> which at times seems triumphantly an extra-
> ordinary kind of wholeness impossible to
> animals and possible only to men on rare
> occasions, is the quality that Roethke has
> caught in his best poems.

This is certainly the quality Dickey seeks in his best poems.

Another poet Dickey praises for a totality of vision is Marianne Moore. He opens a review of *Tell Me, Tell Me* by posing the question: "What poet would we most like to have construct a Heaven for us, out of the things we already have? Construct it from his way of being, his particular method of putting the world together?" His choice is Miss Moore because of her "persuasiveness in getting the things of this world to live together as if they truly belonged that way, and because the communal vividness of her poems suggests to me order of an ideal kind." Her poems have the sense of harmony and the extraordinary vision that Dickey admires. She invites her readers to participate in life by renewing the world in her poetry: Dickey asks, "who knows better than she how sheerly *experienceable* the world is and in how many ways and on how many levels?"

Almost any critic would praise Roethke and Miss Moore, although perhaps not for the same reasons or with the same enthusiasm that Dickey shows. He is as exuberant in his praise about less acclaimed poets, such as Gary Snyder and Galway Kinnell. These poets share with the critic a looser way with cadences, a freer verse and a lack of compression. Besides their experimental approach to form, each has an expansive manner in dealing with his subject. Dickey praises Snyder's poetry because it can "release us to our own waiting, hidden potentialities." Snyder's style, a "musing, drifting series of terse, observant statements," fixes his "experiences and beliefs in such a manner that they become available for us to live among and learn from. And that is the kind of living and learning--within another's life--that we are always hoping poetry will make possible."

Galway Kinnell's poems are notable for "their whole hearted commitment to themselves and...their innocence." Kinnell is like Dickey in his joyous responce to nature and his awareness of the demonic forces in the natural world. Dickey admires the sense of personality in Kinnell's work: "Here you feel quite strongly a genuine presence, an integrated personal reality more powerful and more projected than anything else in recent books except Gary Snyder's poems about logging and fire-watching."

"An integrated personal reality" is perhaps what Dickey values most in poetry. As a critic he measures the poet's world against his own with a liberalness unmarred by consistency. His review of Randall Jarrell is the epitome of considering all the alternatives. The essay is written as a dialogue between A and B. A praises Jarrell for "writing about real things, rather than playing games with words," while B counters that Jarrell clings "like death to the commonplace, as though the Real were only the Ordinary...." and goes on to claim "he has not the power...to make experience rise to its own most intense, concentrated, and meaningful level, a level impossible without *that* poet's having caught it in *those* words." A ends the discussion with the judgment: "He gives you... a foothold in a realm where literature itself is inessential, where your own world is more yours than you could ever have thought, or even felt, but is one you have always known."

The points in this dialogue reveal Dickey's aspirations for poetry: the first is that it should transcend literature and return the reader to his world with a fresh vision of it. B's point that the poet cannot use the ordinary as reality, cannot be content with "brooms, cats, garbage cans, broccoli patches" but must have a personal vision and a new perception of reality to give the reader is a major factor in Dickey's criticism. Part of his charm as a critic is this willingness to contradict himself; he can open a review: "Robert Duncan is certainly one of the most unpityingly pretentious poets I have ever come across" and yet find one of his poems "a visionary statement of obsessing beauty." Dickey's criticism is valuable because he is very specific in what he dislikes and tries to pinpoint the problem; his prejudice toward the active-bardic poet and against traditional forms is offset by an unpretentious manner that admits and explains his bias.

Yet this prejudice does keep Dickey from being the extraordinary critic--the Ezra Pound who could effectively counsel any poet. Rather, Dickey is of the Henry James school; he is cogent and convincing in explaining his own poetic endeavors and in recognizing and advising others. But he fails to appreciate and nourish the poet who is completely different from himself in subject and aspirations. For instance, Richard Wilbur, a poet interested in precision and controlled expression, is praised for his "quietly joyful sense of celebration," yet Dickey sees the "delicious aptness of Wilbur's poems" as a mask for an "unwillingness or inability to think or feel deeply...." J. V. Cunningham is described as "a good, deliberately small and authentic" poet who "concedes entirely too much" to the limitations of traditional verse. Dickey's suspicions of the "bag of monkey-tricks" of poetry prevent him from cherishing a poetry whose end is exactness, compression and the development of rhyme and meter.

In an essay entitled "The Poet Turns on Himself," Dickey examines his own solutions to the technical problems of poetry. As a beginning poet who did not like rhyme because of the "packaged quality," Dickey found the sound he wanted ("an unusual sound of urgency and passion, of grave conviction, or inevitability....") in short anapestic lines in which each line is a declarative sentence. His early poems frequently rely on a refrain with a "strange, incantatory sound" which reflects the dream experiences described in the poetry. As his poems moved out of dream time and into remembered time, Dickey began using a "split line" in which the space between word groups indicated a separateness in the experience.

13

He also turned from the contained, well-made poem to an open or conclusionless poem in the interests of "presentational immediacy." While Dickey's technical ability has been criticized more than any other aspect of his poetry, his discussion of his own poetics reveals that he does practice what he preaches: the form of his poetry grows out of and is secondary to the content.

In a recent review of Dickey's *Poems 1957–1967*, Donald Baker refers to the poet as a "bourgeois American scop." Baker points out that Dickey's poetic cadence depends on the Anglo-Saxon alliterative stress rather than on the lilt of music, but his primary emphasis is on Dickey's style and subject matter. These poems, Baker observes, offer a "suburban mythology,...nostalgic for youth, for home, for the 'heroic' pathos of love, adultery, flying, and sport, for mystic virility, for rebirth into non-human nature, even for death...." James Dickey would not be pleased with the derogatory tone of Baker's review, but he would probably admit that the tag fits his aspirations and his achievement. In a lecture given at the Library of Congress, Dickey spoke of the future of poetry and his belief that poetry should get back "toward basic things and basic-sounding statements about them.... aware all the time that certain constants must be affirmed or not much of life will be worth anything." The constants that Dickey's poetry proclaims are in his own words: "the continuity of the human family, the necessity of both caused and causeless joy, and the permanent interest of what the painter John Marin called 'the big basic forms'--rivers, mountains, woods, oceans, and the creatures that live naturally among them." Like the scop, Dickey affirms these basic things in a poetry which speaks to a wide audience because it expresses funda-

14

mental human experiences.

Since he began publishing poetry in 1951, Dickey's poetry has been popular with layman and specialist. His poetry appears frequently in magazines such as *Life* and the *New Yorker* and just as often in the more specialized *Poetry* and the university quarterlies. Part of Dickey's success depends upon his subject matter; he writes of the ordinary experiences of life--of his family, his piloting experiences in World War II and Korea, and his love of nature, of hunting, camping, and swimming. Another attractive feature is his manner; like Wordsworth, Dickey is a man speaking to men using language heightened by emotion not erudition. Finally, Dickey's appeal rests on his ability to find meaning or consequence in the ordinary experience of here and now. Unlike recent poets, he does not feel the present inferior to the past or feel powerless and humiliated by his position in history. Although Dickey's poetic personae are often turbulent and self-conscious, they are never afraid of life or of appearing vulgar. Dickey, as a poet, tries to immerse himself in life to see "my world as I knew it must be."

If James Dickey had been a seventeenth century poet, he would have sought correspondences with the metaphysicals; in the nineteenth century, he would have celebrated the unity of all things with the transcendentalists. As a twentieth century poet he can find "the double ...meaning of every sensuous fact" and search his own experience for moments that open up the ordinary circumstances of life to a more profound reality. Dickey frequently responds to the infinite life in nature in a way reminiscent of Gerard Manley Hopkins in his joyous sonnets. For instance, the exultant mood of "Hurrahing in Harvest" when the poet senses the divinity inherent in the Welsh landscape and cries out in amazement, "These things, these things were here and but the beholder/ Wanting," is similar to Dickey's sensual awareness of a salt marsh where the poet describes losing himself spiritually as well as physically among the tall stalks of sawgrass. The final stanza of "The Salt Marsh" depicts the poet's inclusion in the scene:

> And nothing prevents your bending
> With them, helping their wave
> Upon wave upon wave upon wave
> By not opposing,
> By willing your supple inclusion
> In their marvelous, spiritual walking
> Everywhere, anywhere.

All of Dickey's poetry aims at the tranquillity of "marvelous spiritual walking," becoming part of the flow of life or learning to "move at the heart of the world." In many poems this communion of nature and man is achieved through the poet's sensitive response to the natural world. In other poems the poet deals with fantastic situations filled with extremes of emotion in which the still point is reached by violence. In order to penetrate the past Dickey depicts a surreal world; dream images are juxtaposed to remembered incidents, time is disordered and the imagined seems more real than the quotidian. "Pursuit from Under," for example, is about a man remembering himself as a child in a southern state who has "read/Myself near the North Pole. In the journal of Artic explorers" and is haunted by his dream of being pursued by a killer whale in the "cold of a personal ice age." The man is left with an image "of how the downed dead pursue us."

Whether leaning toward transcendentalism or surrealism, Dickey's poetry depends on the irrational as much as on the rational mind. In an article about modern poetry in *The Nation*, Louis Simpson discusses "the accelerating movement away from rationalistic verse toward poetry that releases the unconscious, the irrational, or... magic." Simpson points out that "poetic creation has been described by some poets--Wordsworth and Keats come to mind--as a heightened state of consciousness brought about, curiously, by an infusion of the unconscious." Dickey agrees that the poet's perceptions and vision should be heightened so that he can see things with penetrating insight. One of Dickey's poems proceeds from nothing more extraordinary than seeing his family sitting on a screened porch, their shadows spread across the lawn:

> All of them are sitting
> Inside a lamp of coarse wire
> And being in all directions
> Shed upon darkness.
> Their bodies softening to shadow, until
> They come to rest out in the yard
> In a kind of blurred golden country
> In which they more deeply lie
> Than if they were being created
> Of heavenly light.

In the last stanza the people seem

> More than human, and enter the place
> Of small, blindly singing things,
> Seeming to rejoice
> Perpetually, without effort

James Dickey

>   Without knowing why
>   Or how they do it.

Because of the poet's capacity to see with the eyes of his imagination, his world is extended beyond the normal and he can encounter the forces of life "where they more deeply lie."

    While Dickey describes a metamorphosis which gives the spectator, the poet, a new awareness in "A Screened Porch in the Country," in many poems he takes part in the change. The poet, like the oblivious family of the previous poem, immerses himself in the flow of life around him but he forfeits his rational powers in order to gain a new perception. This process is seen most dramatically in a poem about writing a poem entitled "A Dog Sleeping On My Feet." The poem opens with the poet "being the dog's resting place":

>   I turn the page
> Of the notebook, carefully not
>
> Remembering what I have written,
> For now, with my feet beneath him
> Dying like embers,
> The poem is beginning to move
> Up through my pine-prickling legs
> Out of the night wood
>
> Taking hold of the pen by my fingers
> Before me the fox floats lightly,
> On fire with his holy secret.
> All, all are running.
> Marvelous in the pursuit,

Like a dazzle of nails through the ankles,
Like a twisting shout through the trees
Sent after the flying fox
Through the holes of logs, over streams
Stock-still with the pressure of moonlight,
My killed legs,
My legs of a dead thing, follow,

Quick as pins, through the forest
And all rushes on into the dark
And ends on the brightness of paper.
When my hand, which speaks in a daze
The hypnotized language of beasts,
Shall falter and fail

Back into the human tongue,

This poem, according to Dickey, comes not from the intellect but from the poet's exchange of vision with the dog.
H. L. Weatherby, in an article in the *Sewanee Review*, uses this poem to illustrate "the way of exchange" in all Dickey's poetry. He points out that the poet gains immediacy of participation by exchanging his consciousness for that of the beast and that the man's involvement stops the movement of the chase, the stream, the rush and the moonlight "stock-still"; all motion leads to the "brightness of paper." The dog and the man in their composite vision see with perceptions neither could have alone. Dickey's poetry is to be experienced totally--physically, emotionally as well as rationally. The poet invites the reader to bend with the stalks of grass, to see the family metamorphosed and to run with the dog in order "to relate *you*, the unknown but potentially human Other, to the

world that all of us exist in.''

   In one of his poems Dickey humorously contrasts the
imaginative and the humdrum world. The poem ''Chenille''
is ostensibly about bedspreads. There are two types of
chenille bedspreads; those ''you can buy anywhere'':

> They are made by machine
> From a sanctioned, unholy pattern
> Rigid with industry
> They hoard the smell of oil
>
> And hum like looms all night
>   Into your pores, reweaving
> Your body from bobbins

For a restoring sleep there is the other kind of chenille
made by a ''middle-aged man's grandmother'' who ''pulls
the animals through/With a darning needle'' while she
envisions

> Red whales and unicorns,
> Winged elephants, crowned ants:
> Beasts that cannot be thought of
>   By the wholly sane
> Rise up in the rough blurred
> Flowers of fuzzy cloth
> In only their timeless outlines
> Like beasts of Heaven:

It is the individual darning world of fantasy--not the whol-
ly sane bobbins--that approaches heaven. Only those con-
fident in their own vision dare to go beyond the two pea-
cocks of the ordinary chenille to see the way animals

really are.

In his poetry Dickey will not yield to the authority of reason. He wants to transcend the limits of the senses and the boundaries of the material world. One of his methods is to exchange his consciousness with another as he did in "A Dog Sleeping On My Feet"; another method he uses frequently is--quite literally--putting on the being of another. A poem illustrating this is "Approaching Prayer" in which the poet attempts to relive some moments with his dead father whose house he is closing. The poem moves from the poet's desire for communion with his dead father, to the remembrance of a shared hunting scene, to the immersion of himself into the self of the hunted and the hunter, and finally to a sense of being in the heart of the moment. The poem begins with the poet's longing to "go beyond what there is in the room." The rational man cannot find a way to prayer here, so the poet must:

> circle through my father's empty house
> Looking for things to put on
> Or to strip myself of
> So that I can fall to my knees
> And produce a word I can't say
> Until all my reason is slain

The son puts on his father's sweater and finds "two things of my father's/Wild, Bible-reading life"--the spurs of his gamecocks and the head of a boar the son had helped to kill. Strapping the bird spurs to his heels and putting on the hollow hog's head the son kneels down under the attic skylight:

> I draw the breath of life

James Dickey

> For the dead hog
> I catch it from the still air,
> Hold it in the boar's rigid mouth,
> And see
>   A young aging man with a bow
>   And a green arrow pulled to his cheek
>   Standing deep in a mountain creek bed
>   Stiller than trees or stones,
>   Waiting and staring.
> Beasts, Angels

The vision from the Beast's point of view interspersed with the son's reactions lasts until the hog is killed and the son reflects:

> Inside the hair helmet
> I look upward out of the total
> Stillness of killing with arrows.
> I have seen the hog see me kill him
> And I was as still as I hoped.
> I am that still now, and now.
> My father's sweater
> Swarms over me in the dark.
> I see nothing, but for a second
>
> Something goes through me
> Like an accident, a negligent glance
> Like the explosion of a star
> ...
>   I nearly lift
> From the floor, from my father's grave
> Crawling over my chest,

22

As in Emerson's "Brahma" the slayer, slaying, and slain are no longer separate but merge into one. When the son rises to take off his father's things, he can only say:

> I don't know quite what has happened
> Or that anything has
> Hoping only that
> The irrelevancies one thinks of
> When trying to pray
> Are the prayer

In a final section the son compares his vision with those of the prophets who try to answer man's questions:

> In heaven's tongue,
> Using images of earth
> Almightily

In the last stanza the poet gives his manner of approaching prayer, his "means to the hovering place":

> Where I can say only, and truly,
> That my stillness was violent enough,
> That my brain had blood enough,
> That my right hand was steady enough
> That the warmth of my Father's wool grave
> Imparted love enough
> And the keen heels of feathery slaughter
> Provided life enough
> For something important to be:
> That if not heard,
> It may have been somehow said.

James Dickey

Dickey's poetry is, in his own words, "a thousand variations of one song." It is his search for the "self of every substance/As it crouches, hidden and free." In many instances, the poetry focuses on the earth's beasts as a means to the angels, and it is at the intersection of this composite vision that the poet is able to become one with the flow of life around him. In "Approaching Prayer" Dickey put on the animal; in "Springer Mountain" he takes off the man. The poem opens with a hunter standing in the dawn hours watching for the deer until he feels transformed into a deer himself and puts down his "longbow on a branch":

> The buck leaps away and then stops,
> And I step forward, stepping out
>
> Of my shadow and pulling over
> My head one dark heavy sweater
> After another,
> ...
>   The world catches fire
> I put an unbearable light
> Into breath skinned alive of its garments:
> ...
> The green of excess is upon me

By discarding the garments of a man and running with the deer the poet gains a harmony of being:

> For a few steps deep in the dance
> Of what I most am and should be
> And can only be once in this life.

An Introductory Essay

In these two poems one is aware of Dickey's ex-
cesses and how closely they are bound to his virtues.
The poet in a hog's head, fuzzy sweater, and spurs kneel-
ing in an attic is equaled only by the poet running naked
through the forest. Certainly Dickey observes the advice
he gave E. E. Cummings and Richard Eberhart and follows
his own unconventional imagination. At the end of "Spring-
er Mountain" the poet takes into account the preposterous-
ness of the action:

> I limp
> To look for my clothes in the world,
>
> A middle-aged, softening man
> Grinning and shaking his head
> In amazement to last him forever.

This poem gains by an acknowledgment of the af-
fectation. Yet all Dickey's poems abound in histrionic
action and superlative description. In his attempt to push
beyond the boundaries of the senses and matter, the poet
cultivates every excess within the mundane world so that
the inordinate communion or metamorphosis achieved in
the poem will appear possible given these circumstances.
"Approaching Prayer" and "Springer Mountain" are ef-
fective; the energetic and passionate experience of the
poems demands the "willing suspension of disbelief" and
the reader follows the poet into his vision. However in
some of Dickey's poems the poet cannot sustain the in-
tensity. In "Falling," for instance, the action of the
poet is bizarre; a stewardess falls from an airplane and
attempts to convert her death to an air birth through a
marriage with the earth. The poem, however, is too long

25

and the intensity is diffused, and the reader is not engaged.

Dickey believes that empathy is the way into a poem, and it is certainly required for the enjoyment of his. If the reader will not relinquish his skepticism, the poems are merely irrational. When the reader joins the poet in the imagination's extensions of reality, he sees beyond the ordinary.

Dickey's most successful poems share more than strong imagery; all concern love, death and transcendence. The poet's chief concerns are constant; he depicts moments when he feels in accord with the essence of life. Yet his persona has progressed from the frankly autobiographical figure who attempted to lose his form in that of a larger (usually nature) in the early poems, to the spectator of *Buckdancer's Choice* who gains insight from another's experience, to the most recent poems in which the poet wears the mask of a persona in situations farther from ordinary reality.

The enchanting poem "In the Tree House at Night" is typical of Dickey's early poetry because of its reference to one of the poet's brothers who died in childhood and because of the setting in which the poet is peculiarly aware of the natural world. Here the poet gains a feeling of unity with the natural world through the tree house and with the spiritual world through his bond with eternity, his dead brother. In this poem the poet and his brothers, "one dead/The other asleep from much living" are at different stages of consciousness, and they are removed from earth by the tree yet by it connected more closely to the earth. The air, earth, tree and the spirits of the three boys mingle for the poet:

26

I breathe my live brother's light hair.
The blanket around us becomes
As solid as stone, and it sways.
With all my heart, I close
The blue timeless eye of my mind.
Wind springs, as my dead brother smiles
And touches the tree at the root;

A shudder of joy runs up
The trunk; the needles tingle;
One bird uncontrollably cries.
The wind changes round, and I stir
Within another's life. Whose life?
Who is dead? Whose presence is living?
When may I fall strangely to earth,

Who am nailed to this branch by a spirit?
Can two bodies make up a third?
To sing, must I feel the world's light?
My green, graceful bones fill the air
With sleeping birds. Alone, alone
And with them I move gently.
I move at the heart of the world.

The very sound of this poem suggests the floating which
the poem explores. Everything is light, wavering, stirring.
The tree house is a perfect image of the poet's spiritual
state; located half way between heaven and earth, the
house is a part of each. The poet, moving gently between
states of death and life, finds himself alone and yet con-
nected to each, able "to move at the heart of the world"
because of his sense of communion with all life.
The title poem from *Buckdancer's Choice* is named

27

James Dickey

after a song to which the freed slaves once sang and danced. The poem is about the poet's mother, "an old woman...dying of breathless angina" who warbled all day "the thousand variations of one song;/ It is called Buck-dancer's Choice." The ex-slaves, the dying mother and the young boy are brought together in the meaning of the minstrel song. The poet recalls himself standing outside his mother's sickroom:

> Sock-footed, to hear the sounds alter,
> Her tongue like the mockingbird's break
>
> Through stratum after stratum of a tone
> Proclaiming what choices there are
> For the last dancers of their kind,
>
> For ill women and for all slaves
> Of death, and children enchanted at walls
> With a brass-beating glow underfoot,
>
> Not dancing but nearly risen
> Through barnlike, theatrelike houses
> On the wings of the buck and wing.

The freed slave and the dying woman sing their variations of a "song of life" while the boy listens and understands only to claim his version years later. The poem like the original song, celebrates the individual choice which allows the artist to "nearly rise" over the limits of his condition.

From the same volume of poetry, "The Celebration" is remarkable for its central image. Here the poet observes his parents at a carnival and gains a new aware-

28

ness of himself:

> then I saw
> My mother and father, he leaning
> On a dog-chewed cane, she wrapped to the nose
> In the fur of exhausted weasels.
> I believed them buried miles back
> In the country, in the faint sleep
> Of the old,

In the poet's vision they ride the ferris wheel back through time:

> The Wheel of wheels was turning
>
> The colored night around.
> They climbed aboard.

The poet sees them as lovers and recognizes his place:

> Understanding the whirling impulse
> From which I had been born,
> The great gift of shaken lights,
> The being wholly lifted with another,
>
> All this having all and nothing
> To do with me. Believers, I have seen
> The wheel in the middle of the air
> Where old age rises and laughs,
> And on Lakewood Midway became
> In five strides a kind of loving,
> A mortal, a dutiful son.

Dickey celebrates the continuity of the human family. The poet does not expect to find his parents at the carnival; their age and debility are evident. Yet envisioning them on the ferris wheel gives the son a new sense of love, duty and death.

In his most recent poetry Dickey has extended his subject, voice and meter. The poem which opens *Poems 1957–1967* is the longest Dickey has published and resounds with a clarion voice which achieves new dimensions in force and depth through the swelling cadences. Dickey's poem is Whitmanesque in its attempt to embrace all of creation, in its use of apostrophe and catalogue. "A May Day Sermon to the Women of Gilmer County, Ga. by a Woman Preacher Leaving the Baptist Church" contains the familiar themes of love, death and transcendence but it surpasses Dickey's earlier work in its universality and passionate tone. The subject of this poem has been touched on previously in "Cherrylog Road" where a boy tells of his rondezvous with a red-haired country girl whose wrathful, bible-quoting father has threatened her with a flailing. In "May Day Sermon" Dickey enlarges her to a legendary figure who after being thrashed disappears into the spring mist with her lover and becomes part of the local folk lore. The girl and her lover and the recurrent life of springtime are set in contrast to the enraged father who tries to repress her with the holy word. The speaker in the poem is leaving the Baptist Church to worship the rites of spring and life that the girl represents. Her voice is an exuberant mixture of the ranting rhythms of the preacher and the vitality and pulse of spring life.

Dickey links the subject of his poem to nature's own recurrence and repetition through the preacher's reiteration of "Each year at this time...." The poem opens with the announcement:

> Each year at this time I shall be telling you
> of the Lord
> -Fog, Gamecock, Snake and neighbor-giving men
> all the help they need
> To drag their daughters into barns.

In every stanza "each year at this time" is repeated until the final strophe when she says,

> Listen: each year at this time the county speaks
> With its beasts and sinners with its blood: the county
> speaks of
> nothing
> Else each year at this time

The poem is a thundering description of how the county speaks. The "fog, gamecock, snake and neighbor" quoted in the second line of the poem are leitmotivs of spring. The neighbor, often called "sister" or "children," is a witness frequently called upon; the snake is a symbol of lust but also of renewal; the fog is the spirit of spring which lifts and saves the lovers. The gamecock and hen are animal surrogates for the girl and her lover. The life, growth and movement in the earth are shared by animals and men; the activity of all creation is reflected in the joy and pain of the young girl. In the barn where the father screams "like God/And King James as he flails" his daughter, the spiders are "drunk on their threads," the hog's fat is "bristling," gnats "boil," croker sacks are "sprawling and shuttling" and outside at Nickajack Creek fog is taking "the soul from the body of water,"

The strength of the poem is in the oracular tone of the preacher; she is truly possessed by the spirit. Like an Old Testament prophet, she can chant that the young woman was "WHIPPED for the wind in the willow/Tree WHIPPED for Bathsheba and David WHIPPED for the woman taken/ Anywhere anytime...." Her stentorian voice rings out ebulliently in protesting the conflict between the Lord's words and the Lord's land. The girl who hears "the Book speak like a father gone mad: each year at this time will hear the utmost sound/Of herself...." The words only increase her desire to flee with her lover. The preacher exclaims:

Words! Words! Ah, when they leap when they are let out
     of the Bible's
Black Box they whistle they grab the nearest girl
                              and do her hair up
For her lover in root-breaking chains and she knows
                         she was born to hang
In the middle of Gilmer County to dance, on May Day,
                                   with holy
Words all around her with beasts with insects

Finally the evangelist exhorts her "Daughters" to listen and believe the sound of spring, to heed the animals who

                    walk with nothing
To do but be in the spring laurel mist and self-sharpened
Moon walk through the resurrected creeks
                              through the Lord
At their own pace the cow shuts its mouth
                         and the Bible is still

> Still open at anything we are gone the barn wanders
> over the earth.

This poem is the apogee of Dickey's development in style and subject matter. The subject is enhanced by the long loose cadences, the use of exclamations, superlatives and expansive imagery. The joyous celebration of life, the transcendence over time is extolled in a cumulative style which maintains an awesome force and feeling throughout the long poem.

As Dickey's own criticism suggests, Dickey's reader never finds his poetry controlled by form. Rather his poetry grows out of imagery, and his most successful poems are those in which the central situation is powerful enough to evoke dramatic images. His less successful poems fail through a diffuseness when the limpid central image will not sustain and inform the poem.

Dickey is a passionate believer in the power of poetry to intensify and expand life. As a critic he looks for the personal vision and as a poet he aims at finding heaven on earth. He is successful only when the still point has been reached, when the dancer is indistinguishable from the dance. This is an end which cannot be satisfied often and is a minor miracle when it occurs. To Dickey's credit are several of these feats. His final achievement in poetry will rest with his ability to see and respond to "basic things" with a sense of communion and joy. Dickey's poetry lacks the music of Roethke's and the discriminating vocabulary of Moore's, but he enjoys an unusual imagination, an immense energy and vitality and the determination to use them to open up his world.

A. WORKS BY JAMES DICKEY

BOOKS

A1. "Into the Stone." In John Hall Wheelock, ed. *Poets of Today VII*. New York: Charles Scribner's and Sons, 1960, pp. 37–93; Toronto: Saunders and Company, 1960.

A2. *Drowning with Others*. Middletown Connecticut: Wesleyan University Press, 1962; Toronto: Burns and MacEachern, 1962.

A3. *Helmets*. Middleton, Connecticut: Wesleyan University Press, 1964; London: Longmans, 1964; Toronto: Burns and MacEachern, 1964.

A4. *Two Poems of Air*. Portland, Oregon: Centicore Press, 1964.

A5. *The Suspect in Poetry*. Madison, Minnesota: Sixties Press, 1964.

A6. *Buckdancer's Choice*. Middletown, Connecticut: Wesleyan University Press, 1965.

A7. *Poems 1957–1967*. Middletown, Connecticut: Wesleyan University Press, 1967; New York: Collier Books, 1968; Toronto: Burns and MacEachern, 1967.

A8. *Spinning the Crystal Ball*. Washington: Library of Congress, 1967. (20 pages).

A9. *Babel to Byzantium.* New York: Farrar, Straus and Giroux, 1968; Rexdale, Ontario: Ambassador Books, Limited, 1968.

A10. *Metaphor as Pure Adventure.* Washington: Library of Congress, 1968. (20 pages).

A11. *Deliverance.* Boston: Houghton Mifflin, 1970; New York: Dell, 1970.

A12. *The Eye-Beaters, Blood, Victory, Madness, Buckhead, and Mercy.* Garden City, New York: Doubleday, 1970.

A13. *Self-Interviews.* Garden City, New York: Doubleday, 1970.

An Annotated Bibliography

SECTIONS OF BOOKS

A14. "Notes on the Decline of Outrage." In Louis D.
Rubin, Jr. and Robert D. Jacobs, ed. *Modern
Southern Literature in Its Cultural Setting*. New
York: Doubleday, 1961, pp. 76—94. Collected in
Babel to Byzantium.

A15. "Edwin Arlington Robinson: The Many Truths." In
Morton Dauwen Zabel, ed. *Selected Poems of
Edwin Arlington Robinson*. New York: Collier
Books, 1966, pp. xi—xxviii; New York: Macmillan,
1965. Collected in *Babel to Byzantium*.

A16. "The Poet Turns on Himself." In Howard Nemerov,
ed. *Poets on Poetry*. New York: Basic Books,
1966, pp. 225—238. Collected in *Babel to By-
zantium*.

A17. Brief Essays on "A Song to David" by Christopher
Smart; "Dover Beach" by Matthew Arnold; "The
Wreck of the Deutschland" by Gerard Manley Hop-
kins; "The Hound of Heaven" by Francis Thomp-
son; "The Yachts" by William Carlos Williams.
In Oscar Williams, ed. *Master Poems of the Eng-
lish Language*. New York: Washington Square
Press, 1967, pp. 348—350, 750—752, 842—844, 858—
860, 946—948; New York: Trident Press, 1966. Col-
lected in *Babel to Byzantium*.

A18. "Education Via Poetry." *Teaching in America*. Wash-

ington: Fifth Annual Conference of the National
Committee for Support of the Public Schools, 1967,
pp. 34–44.

A19. "Randall Jarrell." In Robert Lowell, Peter Taylor,
and Robert Penn Warren, ed. *Randall Jarrell 1914–
1965*. New York: Farrar, Straus and Giroux, 1967.

A20. An Introduction. In Paul Carroll, ed. *New American
Poets*. Chicago: Follett/Big Table, 1968.

A21. "The Self as Agent." *The Great Ideas Today*, 1968.
Chicago: Encyclopedia Britannica, 1968.

POEMS

1951

A22. "The Shark at the Window," *Sewanee Review*, LIX
(April 1951), 290–291.

A23. "Of Holy War," *Poetry*, LXXIX (October 1951), 24.

1953

A24. "The Child in Armor," *Poetry*, LXXXII (June 1953),
137.

A25. "The Anniversary," *Poetry*, LXXXII (June 1953), 138 –
139.

1954

A26. "The Ground of Killing," *Sewanee Review*, LXII (Oct -
ober 1954), 623–624.

1955

A27. "The Sprinter's Mother," *Shenandoah*, VI (Spring 1955),
17–18.

James Dickey

A28. "Angel of the Maze," *Poetry*, LXXXVI (June 1955), 147–153.

A29. "Confrontation of the Hero (April 1945)," *Sewanee Review*, LXIII (Summer 1955), 461–464.

A30. "The Vigils," *Beloit Poetry Journal*, VI (Fall 1955), 21–23.

1956

A31. "The Flight," *Beloit Poetry Journal*, VI (Summer 1956), 16–19.

A32. "The Father's Body," *Poetry*, LXXXIX (December 1956), 145–149.

1957

A33. "The Swimmer," *Partisan Review*, XXV (Spring 1957), 244–246.

A34. "The First Morning of Cancer," *Poetry*, XC (May 1957), 97–102.

A35. "To Be Edward Thomas," *Beloit Poetry Chapbook*, V (Summer 1957), 10–15.

A36. "The Sprinter's Sleep," *Yale Review*, XXXXVII (September 1957), 72. Collected in "Into the Stone."

A37. "The Red Bow," *Sewanee Review*, LXV (Fall 1957),
627–634.

A38. "The Work of Art," *Hudson Review*, X (Fall 1957),
400–402.

1958

A39. "The Cypresses," *Quarterly Review of Literature*, IX
(Winter 1958), 268–270.

A40. "Poem," *Quarterly Review of Literature*, IX (Winter
1958), 270–271. Collected in "Into the Stone."

A41. "A Beginning Poet, Aged Sixty-Five," *Quarterly Review of Literature*, IX (Winter 1958), 272–273.
Collected in *Drowning with Others* as "To Landrum Guy, Beginning to Write at Sixty."
Reprinted: *Atlantic Monthly*, CCV (May 1960),
69.
Reprinted: *Poems on Poetry*, ed. Robert Wallace and James G. Taaffe. New York: E. P.
Dutton and Company, 1965, p. 239.

A42. "Genesis," *Commentary*, XXV (May 1958), 427.

A43. "Joel Cahill, Dead," *Beloit Poetry Journal*, VIII (Summer 1958), 18–19.

James Dickey

A44. "Dover: Delieving in Kings," *Poetry*, XCII (August
      1958), 283–290. Collected in *Drowing with Others*
      and *Poems 1957–1967*.

1959

A45. "The Other," *Yale Review*, XXXXVIII (Spring 1959),
      398–400. Collected in "Into the Stone" and
      Poems 1957–1967.

A46. "The Vegetable King," *Sewanee Review*, LXVII
      (Spring 1959), 278–280. Collected in "Into the
      Stone" and *Poems 1957–1967*.

A47. "The Jewel," *Saturday Review*, XXXXII (June 6, 1959),
      38. Collected in "Into the Stone" and *Poems
      1957–1967*.
        Reprinted: *The Achievement of James Dickey*,
        Laurence Lieberman. Glenview, Illinois:
        Scott, Foresman, 1968, p. 24.

A48. "The Game," *Poetry*, XCIV (July 1959), 211–212.
      Collected in "Into the Stone."

A49. "The Landfall," *Poetry*, XCIV (July 1959), 213–214.
      Collected in "Into the Stone."

A50. "The Signs," *Poetry*, XCIV (July 1959), 215–218.
      Collected in "Into the Stone."

A51. "The Enclosure," *Poetry*, XCIV (July 1959), 218–220.

42

Collected in "Into the Stone" and *Poems 1957–1967*.

A52. "The Performance," *Poetry*, XCIV (July 1959), 220–221. Collected in "Into the Stone" and *Poems 1957–1967*.
   Reprinted: *Contemporary American Poetry*, ed. Donald Hall. Baltimore: Penguin Books, 1962, p. 77.
   Reprinted: *New Poets of England and America* (Second Selection), ed. Donald Hall and Robert Pack. New York: World Publishing Company, 1962, p. 211.
   Reprinted: *Reading Modern Poetry*, ed. Paul Engle. Atlanta: Scott, Foresman, 1968.
   Reprinted: *The Achievement of James Dickey*, Laurence Lieberman. Glenview, Illinois: Scott, Foresman, 1968, p. 25.

A53. "The String," *Poetry*, XCIV (July 1959), 222–223. Collected in "Into the Stone" and *Poems 1957–1967*.
   Reprinted: *The Achievement of James Dickey*, Laurence Lieberman. Glenview, Illinois: Scott, Foresman, 1968, p. 23.

A54. "Below the Lighthouse," *Poetry*, XCIV (July 1959), 223–224. Collected in "Into the Stone" and *Poems 1957–1967* as "On a Hill Below the Lighthouse."

A55. "Into the Stone," *Poetry*, XCIV (July 1959), 225–226. Collected in "Into the Stone" and *Poems 1957–1967*.

A56. "Awaiting the Swimmer," *Kenyon Review*, XXI (Fall
     1959), 609–610. Collected in "Into the Stone"
     and *Poems 1957–1967*.

A57. "Orpheus before Hades," *New Yorker*, XXXV (Decem-
     ber 5, 1959), 52. Collected in "Into the Stone"
     and *Poems 1957–1967*.

                        1960

A58. "The Call," *Hudson Review*, XII (Winter 1959–1960),
     560. Collected in "Into the Stone."
          Reprinted: *New Poets of England and Amer-
          ica*, (Second Selection), ed. Donald Hall and
          Robert Pack. New York: World Publishing
          Company, 1962, p. 208.

A59. "A Child's Room," *Quarterly Review of Literature*, X
     (Winter 1960), 247–248.

A60. "The Wedding," *Quarterly Review of Literature*, X
     (Winter 1960), 248–249. Collected in "Into the
     Stone" and *Poems 1957–1967*.

A61. "Near Darien," *Quarterly Review of Literature*, X
     (Winter 1960), 249–250. Collected in "Into the
     Stone" and *Poems 1957–1967*.

A62. "The Scratch," *Quarterly Review of Literature*, X
     (Winter 1960), 251–252. Collected in *Drowning
     with Others*.

Reprinted: *American Poetry,* ed. Gay Wilson
Allen, Walter B. Rideout and James K. Rob-
inson. New York: Harper and Row, 1965, p.
1016.

A63. "Uncle," *Quarterly Review of Literature,* X (Winter
1960), 253–254. Collected in "Into the Stone."

A64. "The Island," *Sewanee Review,* LXVIII (Winter 1960),
89–90. Collected in *Drowning with Others.*

A65. "Sleeping out at Easter," *Virginia Quarterly Review,*
XXXVI (Spring 1960), 222. Collected in "Into
the Stone" and *Poems 1957–1967.*
Reprinted: *Reading Modern Poetry,* ed. Paul
Engle. Atlanta: Scott, Foresman, 1968.

A66. "The Underground Stream," *New Yorker,* XXXVI (May
21, 1960), 42. Collected in "Into the Stone" and
Poems 1957–1967.

A67. "The Prodigal," *Poetry Northwest,* I (Spring-Summer
1960), 10–13.

A68. "Walking on Water," *New Yorker,* XXXVI (June 18,
1960), 44. Collected in "Into the Stone" and
Poems 1957–1967.
Reprinted: *New Poets of England and America,*
(Second Selection), ed. Donald Hall and Rob-
ert Pack. New York: World Publishing Com-
pany, 1962, pp. 206–217.

A69. "Trees and Cattle," *New Yorker,* XXXVI (July 16,

1960), 32. Collected in "Into the Stone" and
Poems 1957—1967.

Reprinted: *New Poets of England and America*,
(Second Selection), ed. Donald Hall and Rob-
ert Pack. New York: World Publishing Com-
pany, 1962, p. 209.

A70. "A Birth," *New Yorker*, XXXVI (August 13, 1960), 30.
Collected in *Drowning with Others* and *Poems
1957—1967*.

A71. "Between Two Prisoners," *Yale Review*, L (Septem-
ber 1960), 86—88. Collected in *Drowning with
Others* and *Poems 1957—1967*.

Reprinted: *American Poetry*, ed. Gay Wilson
Allen, Walter B. Rideout and James K. Rob-
inson. New York: Harper and Row, 1965, p.
1014.

Reprinted: *Reading Poetry*, ed. Fred B. Mil-
lett, Arthur W. Hoffman and David R. Clark.
New York: Harper and Row, 1967, p. 143.

A72. "Mindoro, 1944," *Paris Review*, XXII (Autumn-Winter
1960), 122—123. Collected in "Into the Stone."

A73. "Drowning with Other," *Partisan Review*, XXVII (Fall
1960), 636—637. Collected in *Drowning with
Others* and *Poems 1957—1967*.

Reprinted: *A Controversy of Poets*, ed. Paris
Leary and Robert King. New York: Double-
day and Company, 1965, p. 77.

Reprinted: *Reading Poetry*, ed. Fred B. Millett,
Arthur W. Hoffman and David R. Clark. New

York: Harper and Row, 1967, p. 339.

A74. "Autumn," *New Yorker*, XXXVI (October 29, 1960), 42. Collected in *Drowning with Others*.

A75. "Listening to Foxhounds," *New Yorker*, XXXVI (November 26, 1960), 48. Collected in *Drowning with Others* and *Poems 1957–1967*.
Reprinted: *Life*, LXI (July 22, 1966), 70.
Reprinted: *Southern Writing in the Sixties*, ed. John William Corrington and Miller Williams. Baton Rouge: Louisiana State University Press, 1967, p. 13.

A76. "Antipolis," *Poetry*, XCVII (December 1960), 153–154. Collected in *Drowning with Others*.

A77. "View of Fujiyama after the War," *Poetry*, XCVII (December 1960), 156. Collected in *Drowning with Others*.

A78. "Inside the River," *Poetry*, XCVII (December 1960), 156–157. Collected in *Drowning with Others* and *Poems 1957–1967*.

A79. "The Magus," *New Yorker*, XXXVI (December 1960), 30. Collected in *Drowning with Others* and *Poems 1957–1967*.

1961

A80. "The Change," *Kenyon Review*, XXIII (Winter 1961),

71. Collected in *Drowning with Others.*

A81. "Hunting Civil War Relics at Nimblewill Creek,"
Sewanee Review, LXIX (Winter 1961), 139—141.
Collected in *Drowning with Others* and *Poems
1957—1967.*
Reprinted: *Contemporary American Poetry*, ed.
Donald Hall. Baltimore: Penguin Books,
1962, p. 78.

A82. "Facing Africa," *Encounter*, XVI (April 1961), 41.
Collected in *Drowning with Others* and *Poems
1957—1967.*
Reprinted: *Encounter 1953—1963*, ed. Stephen
Spender. New York: Basic Books Inc., 1963,
pp. 551—552.

A83. "Fog Envelops the Animals," *Virginia Quarterly Re-
view*, XXXVII (Spring 1961), 224. Collected in
Drowning with Others and *Poems 1957—1967.*

A84. "The Summons," *Virginia Quarterly Review*, XXXVII
(Spring 1961), 223. Collected in *Drowning with
Others* and *Poems 1957—1967.*

A85. "Via Appia," *Choice*, I (Spring 1961), 50—52.

A86. "In the Tree House at Night," *New Yorker*, XXXVII
(June 24, 1961), 30. Collected in *Drowning with
Others* and *Poems 1957—1967.*
Reprinted: *Today's Poets*, ed. Chad Walsh
New York: Charles Scribner's and Sons, 1964,
p. 290.

Reprinted: *The Achievement of James Dickey,*
Laurence Lieberman. Glenview, Illinois:
Scott, Foresman, 1968, p. 29.

Reprinted: *Poetry: An Introductory Anthology,*
ed. Hazard Adams. Boston: Little, Brown
and Company, 1968, p. 342.

Reprinted: *Faber Book of Modern Verse,* ed.
Michael Roberts and Donald Hall. London:
Faber and Faber, 1965, pp. 373–375.

A87. "The Lifeguard," *New Yorker,* XXXVI (August 5,
1961), 24. Collected in *Drowning with Others*
and *Poems 1957–1967.*

Reprinted: *A Controversy of Poets,* ed. Paris
Leary and Robert Kelly. New York: Double-
day and Company, 1965, p. 69.

Reprinted: *One Hundred American Poems of
The Twentieth Century,* ed. Laurence Per-
rine and J. M. Reid. New York: Harcourt,
Brace and World, 1966, pp. 277–279.

Reprinted: *American Poetry Since 1945,* ed.
Stephen Stepanchev. New York: Harper and
Row, 1965, p. 192.

Reprinted: *The Achievement of James Dickey,*
Lawrence Lieberman. Glenview, Illinois:
Scott, Foresman, 1968, p. 27.

A88. "The Salt Marsh," *New Yorker,* XXXVII (September
16, 1961), 46. Collected in *Drowning with Others*
and *Poems 1957–1967.*

Reprinted: *Life,* LXI (July 22, 1966), 70.

A89. "In the Lupanar at Pompeii," *Kenyon Review,* XXIII

(Fall 1961), 631–633. Collected in *Drowning with Others* and *Poems 1957–1967*.
Reprinted: *Today's Poets*, ed. Chad Walsh. New York: Charles Scribner's and Sons, 1964, p. 292.

A90. "The Movement of Fish," *New Yorker*, XXXVII (October 7, 1961), 58. Collected in *Drowning with Others* and *Poems 1957–1967*.

A91. "In the Mountain Tent," *New Yorker*, XXXVII (October 28, 1961), 54. Collected in *Drowning with Others* and *Poems 1957–1967*.

A92. "The Heaven of Animals," *New Yorker*, XXXVII (November 18, 1961), 48. Collected in *Drowning with Others* and *Poems 1957–1967*.
Reprinted: *The Achievement of James Dickey*, Laurence Lieberman. Glenview, Illinois: Scott, Foresman, 1968, p. 14.
Reprinted: *The Poem in its Skin*, ed. Paul Carroll. Chicago: Follett Publishing Company, 1968, p. 41.
Reprinted: *Faber Book of Modern Verse*, ed. Michael Roberts and Donald Hall. London: Faber and Faber, 1965, p. 372.
Reprinted: *Today's Poets*, ed. Chad Walsh. New York: Charles Scribner's and Sons, 1964, p. 289.
Reprinted: *American Poetry*, ed. Gay Wilson Allen, Walter B. Rideout and James K. Robinson. New York: Harper and Row, 1965, p. 1013.

Reprinted: *Life*, LXI (July 22, 1966), 70.

A93. "For the Nightly Ascent of the Hunter Orion over a Forest Clearing," *New Yorker*, XXXVII (December 2, 1961), 58. Collected in *Drowning with Others* and *Poems 1957–1967*.

A94. "Armor," *Hudson Review*, XIV (Winter 1961–1962), 557–558. Collected in *Drowning with Others*.

A95. "The Owl King," *Hudson Review*, XIV (Winter 1961– 1962), 550–556. Collected in *Drowning with Others* and *Poems 1957–1967*.
Reprinted: *A Controversy of Poets*, ed Paris Leary and Robert Kelly. New York: Double - day and Company, 1965, p. 70.

1962

A96. "Adam in Winter," *Choice*, II (1962), 14–15.

A97. "At the Home for Unwed Mothers," *Quarterly Review of Literature*, XII (Winter 1962), 55–56.

A98. "A Sound Through the Floor," *Quarterly Review of Literature*, XII (Winter 1962), 56–59.

A99. "On Discovering that My Hand Shakes," *Quarterly Review of Literature*, XII (Winter 1962), 59–60.

A100. "The Crows," *New World Writing*, XXI (1962), 50–51.

A101. "Wall and Cloud," *New World Writing*, XXI (1962),
      52.

A102. "A Poem about Bird-Catching by One Who Has Never
      Caught a Bird," *New World Writing*, XXI (1962),
      53—54.

A103. "The Hospital Window," *Poetry*, IC (January 1962),
      236. Collected in *Drowning with Others* and
      Poems 1957—1967.
          Reprinted: *A Controversy of Poets*, ed. Paris
          Leary and Robert King. New York: Double-
          day and Company, 1965, p. 78.
          Reprinted: *Beginnings in Poetry*, ed. W. J.
          Martz. Atlanta: Scott, Foresman, 1965.
          Reprinted: *The Achievement of James Dickey*,
          Laurence Lieberman. Glenview, Illinois:
          Scott, Foresman, 1968, p. 31.

A104. "A Dog Sleeping on my Feet," *Poetry*, IC (January
      1962), 238. Collected in *Drowning with Others*
      and *Poems 1957—1967*.
          Reprinted: *Poems on Poetry*, ed. Robert Wallace
          and James G. Taaffe. New York: E. P. Dut-
          ton and Company, 1965, p. 242.
          Reprinted: *Southern Writing in the Sixties*, ed.
          John William Corrington and Miller Williams.
          Baton Rouge: Louisiana State University
          Press, 1967, p. 13.
          Reprinted: *Reading Poetry*, ed. Fred B. Millett,
          Arthur W. Hoffman and David R. Clark. New
          York: Harper and Row, 1967, pp. 340—341.

A105. "After the Night Hunt," *Poetry*, IC (January 1962), 239–240.

A106. "Gamecock," *Poetry*, IC (January 1962), 240. Collected in *Buckdancer's Choice* and *Poems 1957–1967*.
    Reprinted: *Virginia Quarterly Review*, XXXXI (Spring 1965), 232.
    Reprinted: *Southern Writing in the Sixties*, ed. John William Corrington and Miller Williams. Baton Rouge: Louisiana State University Press, 1967, p. 12.

A107. "Fence Wire," *New Yorker*, XXXVIII (February 24, 1962), 36. Collected in *Helmets* and *Poems 1957–1967*.

A108. "By Canoe through the Fir Forest," *New Yorker*, XXXVIII (June 16, 1962), 32.

A109. "A Letter," *Sewanee Review*, LXX (Summer 1962), 416–417. Collected in *Poems 1957–1967*.

A110. "The Step," *Literary Review*, V (Summer 1962), 474–475.

A111. "Springer Mountain," *Virginia Quarterly Review*, XXXVIII (Summer 1962), 436–441.
    Reprinted: *The Achievement of James Dickey*, Laurence Lieberman. Glenview, Illinois: Scott, Foresman, 1968.

A112. "Below Ellijay," *Poetry*, CI (October 1962), 27–28.

Collected in *Helmets* and *Poems 1957—1967*.

A113. "Poems of North and South Georgia," *New Yorker*, XXXVIII (December 1, 1962), 60—61. Individually titled: "In the Marble Quarry," "The Dusk of Horses," "At Darian Bridge," "The Beholders,' "The Poisoned Men." Collected in *Helmets* and *Poems 1957—1967*.

> Reprinted: "In the Marble Quarry," *Life*, LXI (July 22, 1966), 70; *The Achievement of Jame Dickey*, Laurence Lieberman. Glenview, Illinois: Scott, Foresman, 1968, p. 41.
>
> Reprinted: "The Dusk of Horses," *American Poetry*, ed. Gay Wilson Allen, Walter B. Rideout and James K. Robinson. New York: Harper and Row, 1965, p. 1018; *Today's Poets*, ed. Chad Walsh. New York: Charles Scribner' and Sons, 1964, p. 294; *The Achievement of James Dickey*, Laurence Lieberman. Glenview Illinois: Scott, Foresman, 1968, p. 33.
>
> Reprinted: "The Beholders," *American Poetry*, ed. Gay Wilson Allen, Walter B. Rideout, and James K. Robinson. New York: Harper and Row, 1965, pp. 1019—1020.
>
> Reprinted: "The Poisoned Men," *Today's Poet* ed. Chad Walsh. New York: Charles Scribner's and Sons, 1964, p. 297.

A114. "On the Inundation of the Coosawattee Valley," *Yale Review*, LII (December 1962), 234—235. Collected in *Helmets* and *Poems 1957—1967*.

1963

A115. "The Courtship," *Mutiny*, XII (1963), 96–98.

A116. "Walking the Fire Line," *Mutiny*, XII (1963), 96–98.

A117. "Paestum," *Shenandoah*, XIV (Winter 1963), 4–10.

A118. "Kudzu," *New Yorker*, XXXIX (May 18, 1963), 44.
Collected in *Helmets* and *Poems 1957–1967*.
Reprinted: *Poems of Our Moment: Contemporary
Poets of the English Language*, ed. J. Hollan-
der. New York: Pegasus, 1968.

A119. "The Scarred Girl," *New Yorker*, XXXIX (June 1,
1963), 36. Collected in *Helmets* and *Poems 1957–
1967*.
Reprinted: *Today's Poets*, ed. Chad Walsh. New
York: Charles Scribner's and Sons, 1964, p.
295.

A120. "Drinking from a Helemt," *Sewanee Review*, LXXI
(Summer 1963), 451–457. Collected in *Helmets*
and *Poems 1957–1967*.
Reprinted: *The Achievement of James Dickey*,
Laurence Lieberman. Glenview, Illinois:
Scott, Foresman, 1968, p. 46.

A121. "Why in London the Blind are Saviors," *Poetry*, CII
(August 1963), 284–286.

A122. "The Being," *Poetry*, CII (August 1963), 281–282.

55

Collected in *Helmets* and *Poems 1957–1967*.
Reprinted: *The New Modern Poets*, ed. M. L.
Rosenthal. New York: Macmillan Company,
1967, pp. 44–46.

A123. "A Folk-Singer of the Thirties," *Poetry*, CII (August
1963), 286–291. Collected in *Helmets* and *Poems
1957–1967*.

A124. "Bums, on Waking," *New Yorker*, XXXIX (September
7, 1963), 34. Collected in *Helmets* and *Poems
1957–1967*.
Reprinted: *The Achievement of James Dickey*,
Laurence Lieberman. Glenview, Illinois:
Scott, Foresman, 1968, p. 44.

A125. "Goodbye to Serpents," *New Yorker*, XXXIX (Sep-
tember 21, 1963), 47. Collected in *Helmets* and
Poems 1957–1967.

A126. "Blowgun and Rattlesnake," *Texas Quarterly*, VI
(Autumn 1963), 158–160.

A127. "Horses and Prisoners," *Hudson Review*, XVI
(Autumn 1963), 384–385. Collected in *Helmets*
and *Poems 1957–1967*.
Reprinted: "Best Poems of 1963," *Borestone
Mountain Poetry Awards*, ed. Lionel Steven-
son. Palo Alto, California: Pacific Books,
1964, p. 7.

A128. "In the Child's Night," *Virginia Quarterly Review*,
XXXIX (Autumn 1963), 590–591. Collected in
Helmets.

A129. "Cherrylog Road," *New Yorker*, XXXIX (October 12, 1963), 51. Collected in *Helmets* and *Poems 1957–1967*.
    Reprinted: *Beginnings in Poetry*, ed. W. J. Martz. Atlanta: Scott, Foresman, 1965.
    Reprinted: *The Achievement of James Dickey*, Laurence Lieberman. Glenview, Illinois: Scott, Foresman, 1968, p. 37.

A130. "Breath," *New Yorker*, XXXIX (November 9, 1963), 48. Collected in *Helmets*.

A131. "The Driver," *New Yorker*, XXXIX (December 7, 1963), 54. Collected in *Helmets* and *Poems 1957–1967*.
    Reprinted: "Best Poems of 1963," *Borestone Mountain Poetry Awards*, ed. Lionel Stevenson. Palo Alto, California: Pacific Books, 1964, p. 44.

A132. "The Ice Skin," *New Yorker*, XXXIX (December 28, 1963), 37. Collected in *Helmets* and *Poems 1957–1967*.
    Reprinted: *The Achievement of James Dickey*, Laurence Lieberman. Glenview, Illinois: Scott, Foresman, 1968, p. 42.

1964

A133. "Mary Sheffield," *Shenandoah*, XV (Winter 1964), 52–53. Collected in *Poems 1957–1967*.

A134. "Fox Blood," *Quarterly Review of Literature*, XIII
(Winter-Spring 1964), 37—38. Collected in *Buck-
dancer's Choice* and *Poems 1957—1967*.

A135. "For the Linden Moth," *Quarterly Review of Liter-
ature*, XIII (Winter-Spring 1964), 38—40.

A136. "The Rafters," *Quarterly Review of Literature*, XIII
(Winter-Spring 1964), 40—42.

A137. "Winter Trout," *Paris Review*, XXXI (Winter-Spring
1964), 98—99. Collected in *Helmets* and *Poems
1957—1967*.

A138. "Reincarnation," *New Yorker*, XXXX (March 7, 1964),
51. Collected in *Buckdancer's Choice* and *Poems
1957—1967*.
      Reprinted: *Southern Writing in the Sixties*, ed.
      John William Corrington and Miller Williams.
      Baton Rouge: Louisiana State University
      Press, 1967, pp. 16—17.

A139. "The Second Sleep," *Kenyon Review*, XXVI (Spring
1964), 302—303. Collected in *Buckdancer's Choic*
and *Poems 1957—1967*.

A140. "The Firebombing," *Poetry*, CIV (May 1964), 63—
72. Collected in *Buckdancer's Choice* and *Poems
1957—1967*.
      Reprinted: *Where is Viet Nam? American Poets
      Respond*, ed. Walter Lowenfels. New York:
      Doubleday and Company, 1967, p. 28.
      Reprinted: *The Achievement of James Dickey*,

Laurence Lieberman. Glenview, Illinois:
Scott, Foresman, 1968, p. 52.

A141. "Them, Crying," *New Yorker*, XXXX (May 9, 1964),
42. Collected in *Buckdancer's Choice* and *Poems
1957–1967.*

A142. "The Escape," *New Yorker*, XXXX (July 18, 1964),
30. Collected in *Buckdancer's Choice* and *Poems
1957–1967.*

A143. "Angina," *New Yorker*, XXXX (August 15, 1964), 30 .
Collected in *Buckdancer's Choice.*

A144. "The War Wound," *New Yorker*, XXXX (September
12, 1964), 54. Collected in *Buckdancer's Choice*
and *Poems 1957–1967.*

A145. "The Common Grave," *New Yorker*, XXXX (October
24, 1964), 54. Collected in *Buckdancer's Choice*
and *Poems 1957–1967.*

A146. "Pursuit from Under," *Hudson Review*, XVII (Autumn
1964), 412–414. Collected in *Buckdancer's Choice*
and *Poems 1957–1967.*
Reprinted: *The Achievement of James Dickey,*
Laurence Lieberman, Glenview, Illinois:
Scott, Foresman, 1968, p. 63.

A147. "Faces Seen Once," *Hudson Review*, XVII (Autumn
1964), 414–416. Collected in *Buckdancer's Choice*
and *Poems 1957–1967.*

A148. "Children Reading," *New York Times Children's Book Section*, November 1, 1964, p. 1.

1965

A149. "Sled-Burial, Dream Ceremony," *Southern Review*, I (Winter 1965), 125–126. Collected in *Buckdancer's Choice* and *Poems 1957–1967*.

A150. "The Shark's Parlor," *New Yorker*, XXXX (January 30, 1965), 32–33. Collected in *Buckdancer's Choice* and *Poems 1957–1967*.
    Reprinted: *The Achievement of James Dickey*, Laurence Lieberman. Glenview, Illinois: Scott, Foresman, 1968, p. 60.

A151. "The Fiend," *Partisan Review*, XXXII (Spring 1965), 206–209. Collected in *Buckdancer's Choice* and *Poems 1957–1967*.
    Reprinted: *The Experience of Literature*, ed. Lionel Trilling. New York: Holt, Rinehart and Winston, 1967, pp. 497–500.
    Reprinted: *The Achievement of James Dickey*, Laurence Lieberman. Glenview, Illinois: Scott, Foresman, 1968, p. 65.

A152. "The Night Pool," *Virginia Quarterly Review*, XXXI (Spring 1965), 231–232. Collected in *Buckdancer's Choice* and *Poems 1957–1967*.

A153. "The Head-Aim," *Virginia Quarterly Review*, XXXXI

(Spring 1965), 233–234. Collected in *Poems 1957–1967*.

A154. "The Celebration," *Harper's*, CCXX (June 1965), 50. Collected in *Buckdancer's Choice* and *Poems 1957–1967*.

A155. "Sustainment," *Yale Review*, LIV (June 1965), 547–548. Collected in *Poems 1957–1967*.

A156. "The Aura," *New Yorker*, XXXXI (June 5, 1965), 38. Collected in *Buckdancer's Choice* and *Poems 1957–1967*.

A157. "Buckdancer's Choice," *New Yorker*, XXXXI (June 19, 1965), 36. Collected in *Buckdancer's Choice* and *Poems 1957–1967*.
　　Reprinted: *Reading Modern Poetry*, ed. Paul Engle. Atlanta: Scott, Foresman, 1968.
　　Reprinted: *Poems of Our Moment: Contemporary Poets of the English Language*, ed. J. Hollander. New York: Pegasus, 1968.
　　Reprinted: *The Poem: An Anthology*, ed. Stanley B. Greenfield and A. Kingsley Weatherhead. New York: Appleton-Century-Crofts, 1968, pp. 382–383.

A158. "Deer Among Cattle," *Shenandoah*, XVI (Summer 1965), 78. Collected in *Poems 1957–1967*.

A159. "Mangham," *Kenyon Review*, XXVII (Summer 1965), 476–477. Collected in *Buckdancer's Choice* and *Poems 1957–1967*.

A160. "Slave Quarters," *New Yorker*, XXXXI (August 14, 1965), 28–29. Collected in *Buckdancer's Choice* and *Poems 1957–1967*.

A161. "False Youth: Summer," *Harper's*, CCXXXI (September 1965), 115. Collected in *Poems 1957–1967*.

A162. "Hedge Life," *New Yorker*, XXXXI (September 4, 1965), 34. Collected in *Poems 1957–1967*.

A163. "Coming Back to America," *New Yorker*, XXXXI (September 18, 1965), 57. Collected in *Poems 1957–1967*.

A164. "The Birthday Dream," *The Nation*, CCI (September 27, 1965), 170. Collected in *Poems 1957–1967*.

A165. "Seeking the Chosen," *Times Literary Supplement*, November 25, 1965, p. 1069.

1966

A166. "False Youth: Winter," *New Yorker*, XXXXII (February 26, 1966), 44. Collected in *Poems 1957–1967*.
   Reprinted: *The Achievement of James Dickey*, Laurence Lieberman. Glenview, Illinois: Scott, Foresman, 1968, p. 76.

A167. "Adultery," *The Nation*, CCII (February 28, 1966), 252. Collected in *Poems 1957–1967*.

A168. "For the Last Wolverine," *Atlantic Monthly*, CCXVII
(June 1966), 70–71. Collected in *Poems 1957–
1967*.

A169. "The Bee," *Harper's*, CCXXXII (June 1966), 80–81.
Collected in *Poems 1957–1967*.

A170. "Encounter in the Cage Country," *New Yorker*,
XXXXII (June 11, 1966), 34. Collected in *Poems
1957–1967*.
　　　Reprinted: *The Achievement of James Dickey*,
Laurence Lieberman. Glenview, Illinois:
Scott, Foresman, 1968, p. 75.

A171. "The Sheep-Child," *Atlantic Monthly*, CCXVIII (Au-
gust 1966), 86. Collected in *Poems 1957–1967*.
　　　Reprinted: *The Achievement of James Dickey*,
Laurence Lieberman. Glenview, Illinois:
Scott, Foresman, 1968, p. 69.

A172. "Turning Away," *Hudson Review*, XIX (Autumn 1966),
361–368.

1967

A173. "Sun," *New Yorker*, XXXXII (January 28, 1967), 32.
Collected in *Poems 1957–1967*.
　　　Reprinted: *The Achievement of James Dickey*,
Laurence Lieberman. Glenview, Illinois:
Scott, Foresman, 1968, p. 71.

A174. "Falling," *New Yorker*, XXXXII (February 21, 1967),
    38—40. Collected in *Poems 1957—1967*.
       Reprinted: *Poems of Our Moment: Contemporary
       Poets of the English Language*, ed. J. Hol-
       lander. New York: Pegasus, 1968.
       Reprinted: *The Achievement of James Dickey*,
       Laurence Lieberman. Glenview, Illinois:
       Scott, Foresman, 1968, p. 78.

A175. "Snakebite," *New Yorker*, XXXXIII (February 25,
    1967), 44. Collected in *Poems 1957—1967*.

A176. "Power and Light," *New Yorker*, XXXXIII (March
    11, 1967), 60—61. Collected in *Poems 1957—1967*
       Reprinted: *The Achievement of James Dickey*,
       Laurence Lieberman. Glenview, Illinois:
       Scott, Foresman, 1968, p. 73.

A177. "May Day Sermon to the Women of Gilmer County,
    Georgia, by a Woman Preacher Leaving the Bap-
    tist Church," *Atlantic Monthly*, CCXIX (April
    1967), 90—97. Collected in *Poems 1957—1967*.

A178. "Dark Ones," *Saturday Evening Post*, CCXL (April
    8, 1967), 72. Collected in *Poems 1957—1967*.

1968

A179. "Victory," *Atlantic Monthly*, CCXXII (August 1968),
    48—50. Collected in *The Eye-Beaters*,....

A180. "The Lord In the Air," *New Yorker*, XXXXIV (October 19, 1968), 56. Collected in *The Eye-Beaters*, ...

A181. "The Eye-Beaters," *Harpers*, CCXXXVII (November 1969), 134–136. Collected in *The Eye-Beaters*, ...

1969

A182. "So Long," *Life*, LXVI (January 10, 1969), 22–23. Collected in *The Eye-Beaters*,....

A183. "Knock," *New Yorker*, XXXXIV (January 25, 1969), 92. Collected in *The Eye-Beaters*,....

A184. "The Place," *New Yorker*, XXXXIV (March 1, 1969), 40. Collected in *The Eye-Beaters*,....

A185. "Madness," *New Yorker*, XXXXV (April 26, 1969), 40. Collected in *The Eye-Beaters*,....

A186. "Living There," *Harper's*, CCXXVIII (May 1969), 52–53. Collected in *The Eye-Beaters*,....

A187. "Blood," *Poetry*, CXIV (June 1969), 149. Collected in *The Eye-Beaters*,....

A188. "Diabetes," *Poetry*, CXIV (June 1969), 151. Collected in *The Eye-Beaters*,....

A189. "Under Buzzards," *Poetry*, CXIV (June 1969), 153. Collected in *The Eye-Beaters*,....

A190. "Venom," *Poetry*, CXIV (June 1969), 156. Collected in *The Eye-Beaters*,....

A191. "The Cancer Match," *Poetry*, CXIV (June 1969), 158. Collected in *The Eye-Beaters*,....

A192. "Pine: Taste, Touch and Sight," *Poetry*, CXIV (June 1969), 160. Collected in *The Eye-Beaters*,....

A193. "The Moon Ground," *Life*, LXVII (July 4, 1969), 16c. Collected in *The Eye-Beaters*,....

A194. "Messages," *New Yorker*, XXXV (August 2, 1969), 30. Collected in *The Eye-Beaters*,....

A195. "Looking for the Buckhead Boys," *Atlantic Monthly*, CCXXIV (October 1969), 53—56. Collected in *The Eye-Beaters*,....

A196. "At Mercy Manor," *Atlantic Monthly*, CCXXIV (December 1969), 75—76. Collected in *The Eye-Beaters*,....

1970

A197. "Haunting the Maneuvers," *Harper's*, CCXXX (January 1970), 95.

A198. "Camden Town," *Virginia Quarterly Review*, XXXXVI (Spring 1970), 242—243.

ESSAYS

A199.   "An Old Family Custom," *New York Times Book Review*, June 6, 1965, pp. 1, 16.

A200.   "Robert Frost, Man and Myth," *Atlantic Monthly*, CCXVIII (November 1966), 53—56. Collected in *Babel to Byzantium*.

A201.   "Barnstorming for Poetry," *New York Times Book Review*, January 3, 1967, pp. 1, 22, 23. Collected in *Babel to Byzantium*.

A202.   "The Triumph of Apollo 7," *Life*, LXV (November 1, 1968), 26.

A203.   "The Greatest American Poet," *Atlantic Monthly*, CCXXII (November 1968), 53—58.

A204.   "Comments to Accompany Poems 1957—1967," *Barat Review*, III (1968), 9—15.

A205.   "The poet tries to make a kind of order," *Mademoiselle*, CXXI (September 1970), 142—143. Collected in somewhat different form in *Self-Interviews*.

SHORT STORY

A206.   "Two Days in September," *Atlantic Monthly*, CCXXV

(February 1970), 78–108. An excerpt from
Deliverance.

LETTERS

A207.   *Sewanee Review*, LXIX (Spring 1961), 353–354.
Refers to A217.

A208.   *Sewanee Review*, LXIX (Summer 1961), 512–513.
Another reference to A217.

A209.   "Two Open Letters," *Sewanee Review*, LXXIII
(Winter 1965), 177–178. Refers to A226.

REVIEWS

A210.   "Some of All of It," *Sewanee Review*, LXIV (Spring
1956), 324–348. Reviews: *Selected Poems* by
Randall Jarrell; *The Nightfishing* by W. S. Graham;
The Salt Garden by Howard Nemerov; *The Poems
of Gene Derwood; Book of Moments* by Kenneth
Burke; *Dry Sun, Dry Wind* by David Wagoner; *Figures from a Double World* by Thomas McGrath; *The
Gentle Weight Lifter* by David Ignatow; *Went my
Shepherd* by Howard O. Sackler; *The Moral Circus*
by Edwin Honig. Sections on Jarrell, Nemerov
and Ignatow appear in *The Suspect in Poetry*. Sections on Jarrell, Graham, Nemerov, and Ignatow
appear in *Babel to Byzantium*.

A211. "Five Poets," *Poetry*, LXXXIX (November 1956), 110–117. Reviews: *The Scattered Causes* by Samuel French Morse; *Antennas of Silence* by Ernest Sandeen; *Friday's Child* by Wilfred Watson; *Delta Return* by Charles Bell; *An American Takes a Walk* by Reed Whittemore. Sections on Morse and Whittemore appear in *Babel to Byzantium*.

A212. "From Babel to Byzantium," *Sewanee Review*, LXV (Summer 1957), 508–530. Reviews: *Howl* by Allen Ginsberg; *In the Winter of Cities* by Tennessee Williams; *Poems* by Marica Nardi; *Men and Tin Kettles* by Richard Lyons; *The Battlement* by Donald F. Drummond; *Some Trees* by John Ashberry; *Changes of Garments* by Neil Weiss; *Other Knowledge* by Leonore G. Marshall; *The Center is Everywhere* by E. L. Mayo; *Green Armor on Green Ground* by Rolfe Humphries; *Moon's Farm* by Herbert Read; *Poets of Today III* includes Lee Anderson, Spencer Brown and Joseph Langland; *Villa Narcisse* by Katherine Hoskins. Sections on Ginsberg and Drummond appear in *The Suspect of Poetry*. Sections on Ginsberg, Drummond, Ashberry, Humphries, Read, and Hoskins appear in *Babel to Byzantium*.

A213. "In the Pressence of Anthologies," *Sewanee Review*, LXVI (Spring 1958), 294–314. Reviews: *The New Poets of England and America* ed. by Donald Hall, Robert Pack and Louis Simpson; *Mavericks* ed. by Howard Sergeant and Dannie Abse; *A Case of Samples* by Kingsley Amis; *Poets of Today IV* includes

James Dickey

George Garrett, Theodore Holmes and Robert Wallace; *Letter from a Distant Land* by Phillip Booth; *The Hawk in the Rain* by Ted Hughes; *For Some Stringed Instrument* by Peter Kane Dufault; *When We Were Here Together* by Kenneth Patchen; *Declensions of a Refrain* by Arthur Gregor; *The Strange Islands* by Thomas Merton; *Time without Number* by Daniel Berrigan; *Poems* by Richmond Lattimore; *In Time like Air* by May Sarton; *Poems 1947–1957* by William Jay Smith; *Promises* by Robert Penn Warren; *Great Praises* by Richard Eberhart; *Collected Poems* by Edwin Muir; *Selected Poems* by Lawrence Durrell. Sections on *The New Poets of England and America*, Booth, Patchen, and Eberhart appear in *The Suspect in Poetry*. Sections on *The New Poets of England and America*, Booth, Hughes, Patchen, Sarton, Smith, Warren, Eberhart, Muir, and Durrell appear in *Babel to Byzantium*.

A214. "A Gold-Mine of Consciousness," *Poetry*, LXXXXIV (April 1959), 41–44. Reviews Conrad Aiken's *Sheepfold Hill*. Collected in *Babel to Byzantium*.

A215. "Five Poets," *Poetry*, LXXXXIV (May 1959), 117–123. Reviews: *The Sum* by Alan Stephens; *A Book of Kinds* by Margaret Tongue; *A Local Habitation* by Ellen Kay; *Passage after Midnight* by William Pillin; *The Death of Venus* by Harold Witt. Sections on Kay and Witt appear in *The Suspect in Poetry*. Sections on Tongue, Kay and Witt appear in *Babel to Byzantium*.

70

A216. "The Human Power," *Sewanee Review*, LXVII (Summer 1959), 497–519. Reviews: *Shadow and Wall* by Tania van Zyl; *Certain Poems* by John Edward Hardy; *The Wilderness and Other Poems* by Louis O. Coxe; *Poems* by Emma Swan; *The Night of the Hammer* by Ned O'Gorman; *Third Day Lucky* by Robin Skelton; *The Country of a Thousand Years of Peace and Other Poems* by James Merrill; *The Dark Sister* by Winfield Townley Scott; *Plays and Poems 1948–1958* by Elder Olson; *Poems* by E. E. Cummings; *The Odyssey: A Modern Sequel* by Nikos Kazantzakis. Sections on Ned O'Gorman, E. Olson and Cummings appear in *The Suspect in Poetry*. Sections on Swan, Merrill, Scott, Olson, Cummings and Kazantzakis appear in *Babel to Byzantium*.

A217. "The Suspect in Poetry or Everyman as Detective," *Sewanee Review*, LXVIII (Autumn 1960), 660–674. Reviews *The Sense of Movement* by Thom Gunn; *Portrait of Your Niece and Other Poems* by Carol Hall; *The Clever Body* by Melvin Walker La Follette; *A Lattice for Momos* by R. G. Everson; *Guy Fawkes Night and Other Poems* by John Press; *Apples from Shinar* by Hyam Plutzik; *The Crooked Lines of God* by Brother Antoninus; *The Crow and The Heart* by Hayden Carruth; *The Prodigal Son* by James Kirkup. Sections on Gunn, Antoninus and Carruth appear in *The Suspect in Poetry*. Sections on Gunn, Antoninus, Carruth, and Kirkup appear in *Babel to Byzantium*.

A218. "Five First Books," *Poetry*, LXXXXVII (February 1961), 316–320. Reviews: *Myths and Texts* by

71

Gary Snyder; *To Bedlam and Part Way Back* by
Anne Sexton; *What a Kingdom It Was* by Galway
Kinnell; *The Year of the Green Wave* by Bruce
Cutler; *Bone Thoughts* by George Starbuck. Sec-
tions on Snyder, Sexton and Kinnell appear in *The
Suspect in Poetry*. Sections on Sexton and Kin-
nell appear in *Babel to Byzantium*.

A219. "The Death and Key of the Censor," *Sewanee Re-
view*, LXIX (Spring 1961), 318–332. Reviews:
New and Selected Poems by Howard Nemerov;
Poems 1930–1960 by Josephine Miles; *Outlanders*
by Theodore Weiss; *The Drunk in the Furnace* by
W. S. Merwin; *First Poems* by Lewis Turco; *Won-
derstrand Revisited* by Charles H. Philbrick; *New
American Poetry 1945–1960* ed. by Donald Allen;
Maximus Poems by Charles Olson; *Madonna of
the Cello* by Robert Bagg; *Say Pardon* by David
Ignatow. Sections on Nemerov, Olson and Ignatow
appear in *The Suspect in Poetry*. Sections on
Nemerov, Miles, Weiss, Merwin, Turco, *The New
American Poetry*, Olson, and Ignatow appear in
Babel to Byzantium.

A220. "Confession is not Enough," *New York Times Book
Review*, July 9, 1961, p. 14. Reviews: *Kaddish*
by Allen Ginsberg; *The Maximus Poems* by Charles
Olson; *The Distances* by Charles Olson: *Mountain,
Fire, Thornbush* by Harvey Shapiro. Sections on
Ginsberg and Olson appear in *The Suspect in Po-
etry* and *Babel to Byzantium*.

A221. "Correspondences and Essences," *Virginia Quar-*

terly Review, XXXVII (Autumn 1961), 635–640.
Reviews: *The Many Islands* by William Goodreau;
Apollonian Poems by Arthur Freeman; *Poems and
Translations* by Thomas Kinsella; *Halfway* by
Maxine W. Kumin; *Abraham's Knife* by George Gar-
rett; *Journey to a Known Place* by Hayden Carruth;
West of Your City by William Stafford; *I Am! Says
the Lamb* and *Words for the Wind* by Theodore
Roethke. Sections on Carruth, Stafford and Roethke
appear in *The Suspect in Poetry* and *Babel to By-
zantium*.

A222. "Toward a Solitary Joy," *Hudson Review*, XIV (Win-
ter 1961–1962), 607–613. Reviews: *Skeleton of
Light* by Thomas Vance; *The Bluebells* by John
Masefield; *The Gardener* by John Hall Wheelock;
Poets of Today VIII included Albert Herzing,
John M. Ridland and David R. Slavitt; *The Love-
maker* by Robert Mezey; *The Royal Tiger's Face*
by Marvin Solomon; *The Nets* by Paul Blackburn;
Eighty-five Poems and *Soltices* by Louis MacNeice;
Weep before God by John Wain; *In the Stoneworks*
by John Ciardi; *Versions from Fyodor Tyutchev*
by Charles Tomlinson. Sections on Mezey appear
in *The Suspect in Poetry*. Sections on MacNeice
and Tomlinson appear in *Babel to Byzantium*.

A223. "The Stillness at the Center of the Target," *Sewanee
Review*, LXX (Summer 1962), 484–530. Reviews:
The Unfinished Man by Nissim Ezekiel; *The As-
tronomy of Love* by Jon Stallworthy; *Knowledge
of the Evening* by John Frederick Nims; *The Tree
Witch* by Peter Viereck; *Advice to a Prophet* by

73

Richard Wilbur; *The Opening of the Field* by
Robert Duncan; *Medusa in Gramercy Park* by
Horace Gregory; *The Screens and Other Poems*
by I. A. Richards; *Collected Poems* by Yvor Win-
ters; *A Marianne Moore Reader* by Marianne Moore;
Ghosts of the Heart by John Logan. Sections on
John Logan appears in *The Suspect in Poetry*.
Sections on Nims, Wilbur, Duncan, Gregory, Rich-
ards, Winters, Moore and Logan appear in *Babel
to Byzantium.*

A224. "That Language of the Brain," *Poetry*, CIII (Decem-
ber 1963), 187–190. Reviews Conrad Aiken's
Morning Star of Lord Zero. Collected in *Babel
to Byzantium.*

A225. "First and Last Things," *Poetry*, CIII (February
1964), 316–324. Reviews: *The Imaged Word* by
Rolf Fjelde; *The Hawk and The Lizard* by Gene
Frumkin; *Blind Man's Holiday* by R. G. Everson;
Final Solutions by Frederick Seidel; *Naked as
the Glass* by Jean Burden; *New Poems* by Robert
Graves; *Affinities* by Vernon Watkins; *The Be-
ginning and The End* by Robinson Jeffers; *Col-
lected Poems* by Ralph Hodgson; *The Collected
Later Poems* by William Carlos Williams; *Flowers
of Evil*, revised edition, by Charles Baudelaire.
Sections on Graves, Watkins, Jeffers, Hodgson
and Williams appear in *Babel to Byzantium.*

A226. "Your Next-Door Neighbor's Poems," *Sewanee Re-
view*, LXXII (Spring 1964), 307–321. Reviews:
Imperatives by Anthony Ostroff; *Countermoves* by

Charles Edward Eaton; *The Beginning and The End* by Robinson Jeffers; *Poems 1951–1961* by Robert Hazel; *A Harlot's Hire* by Allen Grossman; *The Obstinacy of Things* by Paul Roche; *Guarded by Women* by Robert Pack; *Selected Poems* by Anne Ridler; *Sun-Stone* by Octavio Paz, translated by Muriel Rukeyser; *Collected Verse Plays* by Richard Eberhart. Sections on Jeffers and Eberhart appear in *Babel to Byzantium*.

A227. "Theodore Roethke," *Poetry*, CV (November 1964), 119–122. Reviews *Sequence, Sometimes Metaphysical*. Collected in *Babel to Byzantium*.

A228. "Orientations," *American Scholar*, XXXIV (Autumn 1965), 646, 648, 650, 656, 658. Reviews: *The Lost World* by Randall Jarrell; *Dream Songs* by John Berryman; *To What Strangers, What Welcome* by J. V. Cummingham; *Selected Poems* by Louis Simpson; *The Wreck of the Thresher and Other Poems* by William Meredith; *A Roof of Tiger Lilies* by Donald Hall; *To Build a Fire* by Melville Cane; *Roots and Branches* by Robert Duncan. Sections on Berryman, Simpson, Meredith, and Duncan appear in *Babel to Byzantium*.

A229. "Edwin Arlington Robinson: The Poet of Secret Lives and Misspent Opportunities," *New York Times Book Review*, May 18, 1969, pp. 1, 10.

B. WORKS ABOUT JAMES DICKEY

BOOKS

B1. Carroll, Paul. *The Poem in Its Skin*. Chicago:
      Follett, pp. 43–49, pp. 210–213.
           A chapter is devoted to "The Heaven of An-
           imals" which is discussed as a typical
           Dickey poem. A biographical sketch of the
           poet is given.

B2. Curley, Dorothy Nyren, Maurice Kramer and Elaine
      Fialka Kramer. *A Library of Literary Criticism:
      Modern American Literature*. New York: Fred-
      erick Ungar, 1969, pp. 287–290.
           Excerpts from critical reviews.

B3. Howard, Richard. *Alone with America*. New York:
      Atheneum, 1969, pp. 75–98.
           An essay dealing with Dickey's development
           from "Orphic utterance" to a "narrative utterly
           without ritual."

B4. Lieberman, Laurence. *The Achievement of James
      Dickey*. Glenview, Illinois: Scott, Foresman, 1968.
           Twenty-four poems are reprinted with a critical
           introduction.

B5. Millett, Fred B., Arthur W. Hoffman and David R. Clark
      Reading Poetry. New York: Harper and Row, 1968,
      p. 143.

Comments and questions are given on "Between Two Prisoners."

B6. Rosenthal, M. L. *The New Poets*. New York: Oxford University Press, 1967, pp. 325–327.
A discussion of "Firebombing" and "The Being."

B6a. Spears, Monroe K. *Dionysus and the City*. New York: Oxford University Press, 1970, pp. 250, 252–260, 269.
Spears' thesis is that modern poetry is Dionysian; Dickey is "distinguished by a very powerful sense of the non-human, mysterious, Dionysian forces in nature."

B7. Stepanchev, Stephen. *American Poetry Since 1945*. New York: Harper and Row, 1965, pp. 190–192.
A discussion of "The Lifeguard."

B8. Waggoner, Hyatt H. *American Poets*. Boston: Houghton Mifflin, 1968, pp. 423, 426–427, 607–610, 613–614.
James Dickey is considered as a critic.

PERIODICAL ESSAYS ABOUT JAMES DICKEY

B9. Bly, Robert. "The Work of James Dickey," *The
Sixties*, VII (Winter 1964), 41–57.
>Critic praises the "spiritual struggle" in
this poetry.

B10. -- "The Collapse of James Dickey," *The Sixties*,
IX (Spring 1967), 70–79.
>Bly suggests that the poet's acceptance of the
values of the establishment have led to his de-
cline. "Repulsive poems" from *Buckdancer's
Choice* are discussed.

B11. Buck, Carol. "The 'Poetry Thing' with James Dickey
Poetry Australia, XXI (April 1968), 4–6.
>An Interview.

B12. Carroll, Paul. "Twenty-five Poets in their Skins,"
Choice, V (Winter 1968), 82–94. [85–86].
>Critic notes Dickey's stunning "sudden ra-
diances of joy and tenderness often mingled
with cruelty, malevolence or violence."

B13. Coulbourn, Keith. "James Dickey: The Poetic Gad-
fly," *The Atlanta Journal and Constitution Mag-
azine*, March 15, 1970, pp. 6–7, 38–43.
>An Interview occasioned by publication of
Deliverance.

B14. Cross, Leslie. "Wisconsin's and America's Poet

of the Year, James Dickey, Talks of his Life and Craft,'' *Milwaukee Journal*, March 20, 1966, Sec. V, p. 4.

An interview occasioned by the NBA for *Buckdancer's Choice*.

B15. Davison, Peter. "Difficulties of Being Major," *Atlantic Monthly*, CCXX (October 1967), 116–121.

James Dickey and Robert Lowell are contrasted as the major American poets.

B16. Dorsey, John. "Overfilling the Image of a Poet," *Baltimore Sun*, March 17, 1968, Sec. D, pp. 1, 3.

James Dickey's poetry is a "celebration of life"; interesting comments on Dickey's pantheism.

B17. Esty, Jane and Paul Lett. "A Mutiny Alert," *Mutiny*, IV (Winter 1961–1962), 3–8. [Refers to A220].

Discussion of Dickey's review of Allen Ginsberg's *Kaddish*.

B18. Flowers, Paul. "Nominations for NBA, 1964," *Memphis Commercial Appeal*, February 7, 1965, Sec. V, p. 6.

This article lists books nominated for the NBA; *Helmets* is listed.

B19. Friedman, Norman. "The Wesleyan Poets," *Chicago Review*, XIX (Fall 1966), 55–66.

Critic believes Dickey not an extraordinary poet but finds his subjects and attitudes interesting.

B20. Goldman, Michael. "Inventing the American Heart," *The Nation*, CCIV (April 24, 1967), 529–530.
   The critic admires the energy and imagery of Dickey's poetry and points out that Dickey has caught the "inhuman American wilderness."

B21. Howard, Richard. "On James Dickey," *Partisan Review*, XXXIII (Summer 1966), 414–428.
   Dickey's use of myth and ritual is examined. A good discussion of Dickey's first two books.

B22. Kizer, Carolyn and James Boatwright. "A Conversation with James Dickey," *Shenandoah*, XVII (Autumn 1966), 3–28.
   Dickey is questioned about a "cult of virile persona" and denies projecting a Hemingway-like personality but declares his "work is almost entirely physical rather than intellectual or mental."

B23. Lieberman, Laurence. "Notes on James Dickey's Style," *The Far Point*, I (Spring-Summer 1969), 57–63.
   Critic examines poet's use of figurative speech in his early work where metaphors are "so closely wedded...to the human events" that they hardly seem figurative. Dickey's innovations in prosody are praised: "the triumph of the split line technique...is the result of... playing off the phrase unit against the hexameter line unit."

B24. "NBA, 1966," *Newsweek*, LXVII (March 28, 1966), 10(

Announcement of *Buckdancer's Choice* as re-
cipient of NBA.

B25. "National Book Awards," *New York Times*, March 16,
1966, p. 42.
Article describing the NBA ceremony.

B26. O'Neil, Paul. "Unlikeliest Poet; with a Sampling of
his Poetry," *Life*, LXI (July 22, 1966), 68, 70, 72,
73, 74, 77, 78, 79.
Biographic attempt to define the poet; good
introduction to Dickey.

B27. Pennington, Bruce and Robert B. Shaw. "James
Dickey," *Harvard Crimson*, November 9, 1967, p. 2.
James Dickey and students talk of poetry and
Life.

B28. "Poet as Journalist," *Time*, XCII (December 13, 1968),
75.
Article on Dickey's assignment covering Apollo
7 flight.

B29. Roberts, Carey. "How James Dickey Views Poetry,"
Atlanta Journal and Constitution Magazine, April
17, 1966, pp. 16, 18.
Poet discusses his southern background.

B30. Robertson, Nan. "New National Poetry Consultant
Can Also Talk a Nonstop Prose," *New York Times*,
September 10, 1966, Sec. I, p. 11.
At a news conference on assuming duties as
poetry consultant, Dickey describes his manner

of writing "late at night, early in the morning, at home, on buses...."

B31. Skinner, Olivia. "A Muscular Exponent of Poetry," *St. Louis Post-Dispatch*, November 15, 1967, Sec. F, p. 2.
   General interview.

B32. Tulip, James. "Robert Lowell and James Dickey," *Poetry Australia*, No. 24 (October 1968), 38–47.
   The critic contrasts the attitudes of the poets and discusses their poetry.

B33. Weatherby, H. L. "Way of Exchange in James Dickey's Poetry," *Sewanee Review*, LXXIV (Summer 1966), 669–680.
   "A Dog Sleeping on My Feet" is used to illustrate the "way of exchange" in all Dickey's poetry.

BOOK REVIEWS

"INTO THE STONE"

B34. Baro, Gene. "The Sound of Three New Poetic Voices,"
New York Herald Tribune Book Review, October 30,
1960, p. 10.
> Critic praises Dickey's poems as "metaphysical
> dramas."

B35. Burke, Herbert. *Library Journal*, LXXXV (September
1, 1960), 2947.
> "Highly recommended."

B36. Evans, Oliver. "University Influence on Poetry,"
Prairie Schooner, XXXV (Summer 1961), 179–180.
> Critic notes narrow frame of reference, impre-
> cise epithet and infelicitous sound effects yet
> "also talent is there."

B37. K., N. D. *San Francisco Chronicle*, November 6,
1960, *This World Magazine Weekly*, p. 35.
> Critic notes a "poetry in stoccato, three beat
> lines" dealing with "intense personal experi-
> ences."

B38. Thompson, John. "A Catalogue of Poets," *Hudson
Review*, XIII (Winter 1960–1961), 618–625. [623].
> Reviewer finds poet "very imaginative, even
> fanciful," war poems are "most memorable."

B39. Wright, James. "Shelf of New Poets," *Poetry*, IC
       (December 1961), 178–183. [178–180].
          Critic lauds poetry for embodying a "confron-
          tation of some of the most difficult and impor-
          tant experiences that a human being can have."

DROWNING WITH OTHERS

B40. Allen, Morse. "Modern Poets," *Hartford Courant*,
       May 20, 1962, *Magazine*, p. 14.
          Short review in which critic notes that Dick-
          ey's "imagination expands little incidents
          into large significance."

B41. Flint, R. W. "Poetry Chronicle," *Partisan Review*,
       XXIX (Spring 1962), 290–292. [292].
          This Yankee reviewer is "struck dumb by
          James Dickey's deep-Dixie spiritual approach."

B42. Francis, H. E. "Dickey Shows New Growth in Mean-
       ing Chant," *Atlanta Journal-Constitution*, February
       25, 1962, Sec. D, p. 6.
          Praise for Dickey's ability to see "the infinite
          in the infinitesimal, the Godness in man and
          things."

B43. Gunn, Thomas. "Things, Voices, Minds," *Yale Re-
       view*, LII (Autumn 1962), 129–138. [131].
          Gunn comments on Dickey's images and use of
          "sharp, precise, hard words in descriptions"
          and notes two weaknesses: "monotonous"

meter and "the distrust of conceptual language."

B44. Howard, Richard. "Five Poets," *Poetry,* CI
(March 1963), 412–418. [415].
Lauds "remarkable book" of "fresh exciting
poetry;" finds it reminicent of Thomas and
Roethke.

B45. K., H. A. *Boston Sunday Globe,* March 25, 1962, Sec.
A, p. 57.
Lauds Dickey as "master of quiet mood and
quiet music in indentification with nature."

B46. Kennedy, X. J. "Some Times It's the Sound That
Counts," *New York Times Book Review,* July 15,
1962, p. 4.
"Expectedness of diction" is a fault here;
images that "reward the ear" are noted.

B47. Korges, James. "James Dickey and Other Good Poets,"
Minnesota Review, III (Summer 1963), 473–491.
[491].
"The poems of James Dickey are the work of
a major talent in a genius." Good discussion
of Dickey's imagery.

B48. Lask, Thomas. "Voice of the Poet," *New York Times
Book Review,* December 2, 1962, p. 47.
Critic praises spacing of lines which "gives
sudden movement" and breaks into "declamation
of high order."

B49. Logan John. "Poetry Shelf," *The Critic*, XXI (December-January 1962–1963), 84–85. [84].

> Praise for "mighty, controlled, formal" poetry.

B50. Morse, Samuel French. "A Baker's Dozen?" *Virginia Quarterly Review*, XXXVIII (Spring 1962), 324–330. [324].

> Dickey's poetry is "excellent and original." His characteristic theme is "one of identity."

B51. -- "Poetry 1962: A Partial View," *Wisconsin Studies in Contemporary Literature*, IV (Autumn 1963), 367–380. [371–372].

> Critic praises collection but finds "long poems less sustained than short."

B52. Nemerov, Howard. "Poems of Darkness and a Specialized Light," *Sewanee Review*, LXXI (Winter 1963), 99–104.

> Generous review: critic points out "some brilliant accomplishments here" and also something "I don't respond to, that I don't understand."

B53. Owen, Guy. *Books Abroad*, XXXVI (Summer 1962), 324.

> "Recommended without reservation."

B54. Schevill, James. "Experience in Image, Sound, and Rhythm," *Saturday Review*, XXXXV (May 5, 1962), 24.

> "Gifted James Dickey presents a fresh approach to nature" yet at times a "too easy surface mysticism."

B55. Silverstein, Norman. "Two Modes of Despair,"*Spirit,* XXIX (September 1962), 122.
     Critic finds that Dickey "sacramentalizes his world."

B56. Simon, John. "More Brass than Enduring," *Hudson Review,* XV (Autumn 1962), 455–468. [466–467].
     High praise for "a major talent." "Poem after poem unabatingly good."

HELMETS

B57. Berry, Wendell. "James Dickey's New Book," *Poetry,* CV (November 1964), 130–131.
     Critic finds "galloping rhythms" are "dulling and aggravating."

B58. *Booklist,* LXIII (June 1, 1967), 1027.
     "A gifted articulate poet knows and loves but doesn't romanticize the rural American south."

B59. Bornhauser, Fred. "Poetry by Poem," *Virginia Quarterly Review,* XXXXI (Winter 1965), 146–152. [149] .
     Critic lauds "fresh vision" but objects to "senseless arbitrary" spacing of lines and "droning" anapests.

B60. Burns, R. K. *Library Journal,* LXXXIX (March 1, 1964), 1095.
     Reviewer finds "subjects like the steel hat: rugged, simple and noble."

B61.   *Choice*, II (May 1965), 157.
       "This poetry is essential to modern American
       poetry studies."

B62.   *Country Beautiful*, IV (August 1965), 73.
       "*Helmets* supports the belief that James Dickey
       has the most promising talent of the generation
       coming to poetic maturity."

B63.   Donoghue, Denis. "The Good Old Complex Fate,"
       Hudson Review, XVII (Summer 1964), 267–277.
       [274].
       The critic applauds the collection especially
       " The Scarred Girl,"--"one of the finest short
       poems of the century."

B64.   Flint, R. W. "Three American Poets," *New York Re-*
       view of Books, June 25, 1964, pp. 13–14.
       Reviewer calls Dickey "outdoor poet and a
       Phenomenon." Recommends "Cherrylog Road."

B65.   Harrison, Keith. "Disappointments," *Spectator*, No.
       7108 (September 18, 1964), 375.
       Critic commends the "texture" and "musical
       unity" of poems.

B66.   Kennedy, X. J. "Joys, Grief and All Things Innocent,
       Hapless, Forsaken," *New York Times Book Review*,
       August 23, 1964, p. 5.
       Helmets is Dickey's best work so far. "It is
       rich in relentless intelligence that has made
       him the finest of our new critics of poetry."

B67. Lieberman, Laurence. "Poetry Chronicle: Last
Poems, Fragments and Wholes," *Antioch Review*,
XXIV (Winter 1964), 537–543. [541].
James Dickey is praised for evolving a poetic
line that "works wonders in the extended lyric."

B68. Martz, Louis L. "Recent Poetry: The Elegiac Mode,"
Yale Review, LIV (December 1964), 285–298. [289].
Critic lauds the format of Dickey's poetry.
"Poems tend to open with a taste of actual
world around us and then move on into a trans-
cendent vision...."

B69. Meiners, R. K. "The Necessary and Permanent Rev-
volution," *Southern Review*, N.S., I (Autumn 1965),
926–944. [940].
Critic is annoyed by Dickey's "insistent meta-
phors" yet praises Dickey as best "of poets of
new style."

B70. Meredith, William. "James Dickey's Poems," *Par-
tisan Review*, XXXII (Summer 1965), 456–457.
Applause for poetry which rises from experience--
"the facts of his poems demand a poem."

B71. Morse, Samuel French. "Poetry, 1964," *Wisconsin
Studies in Contemporary Literature*, VI (Autumn
1965), 354–367. [356].
A brief comment noting a "memorable achieve-
ment."

B72. Owen, Guy. *Books Abroad*, XXXIX (Winter 1965), 94.
"A highly original and memorable volume."

B73. Ricks, Christopher. "Spotting Syllabies," *New
      Statesman*, LXVII (May 1, 1964), 685.
            Critic acknowledges "the poet" but objects
      to "spilling and sliding rhythm."

B74. "Rustic and Urbane," *Times Literary Supplement*,
      August 20, 1964, p. 78.
            James Dickey has a "delicate eye for natural
      beauty," however, "promising situations dif-
      fuse rather than transform."

B75. Turco, Lewis. "The Suspect in Criticism," *Mad
      River Review*, I (Spring 1965), 81–85.
            Helmets is "darkly mysterious...mumbling...
      monotonous."

TWO POEMS OF AIR

B76. Duncan, Robert. "Oriented by Instinct by Stars,"
      Poetry, CV (November 1964), 131–133.
            Critic praises spectral poems, notes "a more
      casual verse."

B77. Kennedy, X. J. "Joys, Grief and All Things Innocent,
      Hapless, Forsaken," *New York Times Book Review*,
      August 23, 1964, p. 5.
            These poems are like "personal letters from
      an archangel."

B78. Scarbrough, George. "One Flew East, One Flew West,
      One Flew Over the Cuckoo's Nest," *Sewanee Review*,

LXXIII (Winter 1965), 138–150. [138–141].
"The book seemed in flight in my hands as I
read. The second poem is less moving but
descriptions are more beautiful."

BUCKDANCER'S CHOICE

B79. Bennett, Joseph. "A Man with a Voice," *New York
Times Book Review*, February 6, 1966, p. 10.
"One of the remarkable books of the decade."
"Firebombing," "Slave Quarters" and "Fiend"
discussed in detail.

B80. *Booklist*, LXII (December 1, 1965), 350.
"The presence of death...is the chief pre-
occupation of a disciplined poet...."

B81. *Choice*, III (October 1966), 636.
"This should be in all poetry collections."

B82. Dickey, William. "The Thing Itself," *Hudson Review*,
XIX (Spring 1966), 146–155. [154].
Critic finds "sense of motion, of engagement"
dominating this book and praises the poet for
his ability to juxtapose present and past or
reality and dream in a tense relationship.

B83. Hochman, Sandra. "Some of America's Most Natural
Resources." *Book Week*, February 20, 1966, p. 4.
Dickey is poet-prophet. "Firebombing" likened
to fire sermons of T. S. Eliot.

B84. Huff, Robert. "The Lamb, The Clocks, The Blue Light," *Poetry*, CIX (October 1966), 46–48.
Critic names "Firebombing" "best poem of World War II." *Buckdancer's Choice* is "strikingly guilt-ridden book."

B85. Ignatow, David. "The Permanent Hell," *The Nation*, CCII (June 20, 1966), 752–753.
Interesting discussion of "The Firebombing" and comparison of Dickey and Walt Whitman.

B86. Monagham, Charles. *Commonweal*, LXXXIV (April 15, 1966), 120.
"This is the finest volume of poetry to appear in the sixties."

B87. Morse, Samuel French. "Poetry, 1965," *Wisconsin Studies in Contemporary Literature*, VII (August 1966), 336–355. [349].
"*Buckdancer's Choice* in a transitional volume." Poems criticized for "uneasiness of expectancy."

B88. Strange, W. C. "To Dream, To Remember: James Dickey's *Buckdancer's Choice*," *Northwest Review*, VII (Fall-Winter 1965–1966), 33–34.
Poems divided into "dream" and "remembered" poems. Critic prefers remembered. Good discussion of "The Celebration" and title poem.

B89. *Kirkus*, XXXIII (August 1, 1965), 797.
Critic praises narrative poems yet finds "changes from stanzaic to free floating form not completely satisfactory."

92

B90. *Virginia Quarterly Review*, XXXXII (Summer 1966), xciv.

> Dickey's "best book so far." These poems probe a baffling and uncertain world.

POEMS 1957–1967

B91. Baker, Donald W. "The Poetry of James Dickey," *Poetry*, CXI (March 1968), 400–401.

> Critic notes "recurrent slickness and sentimentality," calls Dickey "bourgeois American scop."

B92. Corrington, John William. "James Dickey's *Poems 1957–1967*: A Personal Appraisal," *Georgia Review*, XXII (Spring 1968), 12–23.

> High praise for poet of "strange and encompassing vision." Detailed discussion of "Adultery," "Folk-Singer of the Thirties" and "Hunting Civil War Relics."

B93. *Choice*, IV (October 1967), 824.

> "Required reading."

B94. Daniel, Rosemary. "Former Atlantan Hymns the Divinity of Existence," *Atlanta Journal*, April 23, 1967, Sec. B, p. 10.

> "James Dickey writes of all aspects of life with great talent."

B95. Davis, D. M. "Four Volumes Prove That Lyric Poetry Survives," *National Observer*, July 10, 1967, p. 19.

Critic praises "new line" in Dickey's poetry and likens to Anglo-Saxon poetry.

B96.   Flanigan, Marion. "300 Poems by James Dickey," *Providence Sunday Journal*, May 21, 1967, Sec. W, p. 20.

Critic considers James Dickey's artistry high for volume of 300 poems; volume has 106 poems, 300 pages.

B97.   Fuller, Edmund. "The Bookshelf: Poets of Affirmation," *Wall Street Journal*, May 24, 1967, p. 16. James Dickey named "the most fertile, powerful American poet currently practicing."

B98.   Garrigue, Jean. "James Dickey, Airborne and Earthbound," *New Leader*, L (May 22, 1967), 21–23. Poet-critic rhapsodizes "James Dickey treads air, trying to say the impossible."

B99.   Grossman, Allen. "Dream World of James Dickey," *Boston Sunday Globe*, April 2, 1967, Sec. B, p. 33.

Reviewer finds the major subject here is the "uncanny spectacle of things changing from one state to another."

B100. Jones, Marion. "Dickey's Works Range All Emotions," *Hartford Times*, May 12, 1967, Sec. D, p. 24. Critic notes change in poetry: "The original James Dickey was a little spirit burdened with the reality of life: 'Faces seen once.' The new James Dickey is a devastating and powerful force.

B101. "Leaps and Plunges," *Times Literary Supplement,*
  May 8, 1967, p. 430.
>   Faint praise: "Dickey has talent certainly but
>   not great or major."

B102. L'Heureux, John. "Having a Beer with One's Soul,"
  Boston Sunday Herald, June 4, 1967, Show Guide,
  p. 19.
>   "The Last Wolverine" is selected as Dickey at
>   his best. "James Dickey attempts a religious
>   secularity which accepts the glory and boredom
>   of a world left on its own."

B103. Lieberman, Laurence. "The Worldly Mystic," *Hudson Review,* XX (August 1967), 513–519.
>   A discussion of the persona of the poems-a man
>   of two worlds who makes "himself and his art
>   a medium...through which the opposed worlds...
>   can meet and connect...."

B104. -- "The Expansional Poet: A Return to Personality, "
  Yale Review, LVII (Winter 1968), 258–272.
>   Dickey's personae in these poems are more in-
>   tense; they are "self-transcendent dream-beings"
>   through whom the poet "plunges into an unfamil-
>   liar field of experience."

B105. Meiners, R. K. "The Way Out: The Poetry of Delmore
  Schwartz and Others," *The Southern Review,* VII
  (Winter 1971), 318–320.
>   Critic lauds Dickey as "an exciting poet" but
>   laments his "extravagant rhetoric."

B106. Meredith, William. "A Good Time for All," *New York Times Book Review*, April 23, 1967, p. 4.
"The best of Dickey's poems achieve living characterizations," yet "his work has the flaws of bardic vulgarity."

B107. Mills, Ralph J. Jr. "The Poetry of James Dickey," *Triquarterly*, XI (Winter 1968), 231–242.
Mills praises Dickey's "large capacity for feeling, for steeping his spirit in the being of others and in the very life of creation" but also notes a recent "diminishing of Dickey's poetic intensity."

B108. Morris, Harry. "A Formal View of the Poetry of Dickey, Garrigue, and Simpson," *Sewanee Review*, LXXVII (Spring 1969), 318–325.
The critic condemns Dickey's lack of conciseness, neglect of traditional forms, lack of verbal precision, and errors about rattlesnakes.

B109. Nolan, James W. "Poetry Not What It Once Was," *New Orleans Times Picayune*, June 11, 1967, Sec. III, p. 4.
James Dickey is hailed as an "exponent of a new directness."

B110. Nash, Jay Robert. "From the Publisher," *Literary Times*, IV (May-June 1967), 9.
"James Dickey's voice will cry loudest and perhaps longest in the next decade."

B111. Pryce-Jones, Alan. "An Exception to the Rule on

Poets," *New York World Journal Tribune,* April 27, 1967, p. 29.

>   Reviewer discusses Dickey's gift for extension."
>   He "worries a theme as a dog worries a bone."

B112. Simon, John. *Commonweal,* LXXXVII (December 1, 1967), 315.

>   "This is one of our most untrammeled, irrepressible, yet never formless poets. I place James Dickey squarely above Lowell."

B113. Simpson, Louis. "New Books of Poems," *Harper's,* CCXXXV (August 1967), 89–91. [90].

>   "Dickey creates a poem that enlarges our experience." Critic praise originality, energy but points out occasional "fabrication of emotions."

B114. Squires, Radcliffe. "James Dickey and Others," *Michigan Quarterly Review,* VI (Fall 1967), 296–298. [297].

>   "In the past five years James Dickey has brought off a one man revolution against the small, the timid the baroquely ordered poem. He insists on the largeness of experience, the aggressiveness of action."

B115. Stanford, Ann. "Poet of Palpitating Hearth," *Los Angeles Times,* April 23, 1967, *Calendar Magazine,* p. 28.

>   This book represents "ten years of astonishing productivity by a talented and impressive poet."

B116. Symons, Julian. "Moveable Feet," *New Statesman*, LXXIII (June 16, 1967), 849.

    The "heresy" of Pound and Williams has led to the "unreadable" poetry of James Dickey.

B117. Tillinghast, Richard. "Pilot into Poet," *New Republic*, CLVII (September 9, 1967), 28–29.

    A close look at "Firebombing" and "Slave Quarters"; poems "relevant" to America today.

B118. "Trade Reviews," *Antiquarian Bookman*, XXXIX (April 10, 1967), 1501.

    "All kinds of poetry here: soft gutsy, color, smell, sight and most of all physical feeling made into words, intellectual but not at all sterile."

B119. Untermeyer, Louis. "A Way of Seeing and Saying," *Saturday Review*, L (May 6, 1967), 31.

    "This is the poetry book of the year." Discussion of Dickey's "unique" vision and "utterance."

B120. *Virginia Quarterly Review*, XXXXIII (Autumn 1967), clxviii.

    Dickey is a "raucous, Brobdingnagian poet;" his work is "massively blemished, sprawlingly disordered; its disorder stems from haste not art."

B121. Wolff, Geoffrey A. "Poet on a Motorcycle," *The Washington Post*, May 9, 1967, Sec. A, p. 22.

Reviewer enjoys Dickey's writing about machines. He describes magnificently the broken cars...and his apostrophes to the technical beauty of airplanes are unequaled.''

THE EYE-BEATERS, BLOOD, VICTORY, MADNESS, BUCKHEAD, AND MERCY

B122. Demott, Benjamin. " 'The More Life School' of James Dickey,'' *Saturday Review*, LIII (March 28, 1970), 25.
    The poetry is ''death-obsessed, dense with assault and pain.'' ''A first rate Dickey poem breathes the energy of the world....To read him is...to share that capacity.''

B123. Howard, Richard. ''Resurrection for a Little While,'' *The Nation*, CCX (March 23, 1970), 341–342.
    An excellent discussion of this volume and of Dickey's recurrent themes.

DELIVERANCE

B124. Algren, Nelson. ''Trickey Dickey,'' *Critic*, XXVIII (May-June 1970), 77–79.
    Critic doubted poet's ability to sustain a novel and was not prepared for the ''cry of the void into which *Deliverance* swept me.''

B125. Bedient, Calvin. "Gold-Glowing Mote," *The Nation*, CCX (April 6, 1970), 407—408.
"Where *Deliverance* attempts conscience depth, a moral or a biting conception, it promises more than it delivers...and yet there stirs within this paper cage...a mountain lion of a tale--direct, brutal and staggering.

B126. Connell, Evan S. Jr. *The New York Times Book Review*, March 22, 1970, p. 1.
"...the story is absorbing, even when you are not quite persuaded Dickey has told the truth. He is effective, and he is deft, with the fine hand of an archer."

B127. Demott, Benjamin. " 'The More Life' School and James Dickey," *Saturday Review*, LIII (March 28, 1970), 25.
Critic faults Dickey for avoiding the contest between Medlock and Gentry in the novel by having the more-life hero incapacitated and the ordinary man take over.

B128. Gray, Paul Edwards. "New Fiction in Review," *Yale Review*, LIX (Autumn 1970), 104—105.
"A primal fable of intense power,"

B129. Keller, Marcia. *The Library Journal*, LXXXXV (May 15, 1970), 1969.
"Compelling reading."

B130. Marsh, Pamela. "James Dickey: Violent on Violence," *Christian Science Monitor*, LXII (April 2, 1970), 7.

"Mr. Dickey's message is horrifying--and so is his medium."

B131. Ricks, Christopher. "Man Hunt," *The New York Review of Books*, XIV (April 23, 1970), 40.
"*Deliverance* is too patently the concoction of a situation in which it will be morally permissible...to kill men with a bow and arrow."

B132. Rosenthal, Lucy. "A novel of man, the forest, death and heroism," *Book World*, IV (March 15, 1970), 1.
"This is both an absorbing--for its poetic-novelistic pioneering--and an important book."

B133. Samuels, Charles Thomas. "What hath Dickey Delivered?" *The New Republic*, CLXII (April 18, 1970), 23–26.
Reviewer finds "latent homosexuality and symbolic transference" at the base of the novel.

B134. Sissman, L. E. "Poet into Novelist," *The New Yorker*, XXXXVI (May 2, 1970), 123.
"Mr. Dickey has discharged his responsibilities as a first novelist with power, skill and grace."

B135. Stone, Robert. "Adrift in our ancestral jungle," *Life*, LXVIII (March 27, 1970), 10.
"In *Deliverance* Dickey finds and renders a quality of terror in the struggle of human against human sufficient to chill the most complacent heart."

B136. *Time*, LXXXXV (April 20, 1970), 92.

> *Deliverance* is compared to *Heart of Darkness*
> and *The Bear*, yet at the crucial moment this
> novel fails: "no single action is impossible to
> believe, but the accumulation...is...too much.

B137. *The Virginia Quarterly Review*, XXXVI (Summer 1970)
lxxxviii.
> "Venerable narrative devices are employed with
> conspicuous success."

B138. Wolf, Gregory. *Best Sellers*, XXX (April 1, 1970),
11–12.
> Critic finds Dickey's faith in the imagination's
> ability to convert any experience into "lifesaving
> ness" sustaining the novel as it does the poetry.

B139. Wolff, Geoffrey. "Hunting in Hell," *Newsweek*, LXX
(March 30, 1970), 94B.
> "*Deliverance* has two central obsessions.... The
> first is the matter of ritual and in this Dickey
> resembles Hemingway....The second is with the
> superman. The fit survive....the weak perish....
> a remarkable tale."

B140. Yoder, Ed. *Harper's*, CCXXXX (April 1970), 106.
> "...believable--with all its faults a wholly
> absorbing tale."

SELF-INTERVIEWS

B141. Petty, Roy. "How Art Gets Made," *Book World*, April

25, 1971, pp. 8—9.
"The [tape recorder] method makes the book a
little long-winded, but it accomplishes the in-
tended purpose of revealing clearly and honestly
how the poet thinks and works."

B142. Yardley, Jonathan. "More of Superpoet," *The New
Republic*, CLXIII (December 5, 1970), 26—27.
"*Self-Interviews* does not really do what it
promises"; however the section dealing with
the poetry is "more helpful." "An interesting
piece of work."

THE SUSPECT IN POETRY

B143. "Bookmarks," *Prairie Schooner*, XXXIX (Summer
1965), 176.
"Reviews should not be published in book form."

B144. Dickey, William. "Talking about What's Real," *Hud-
son Review*, XVIII (Winter 1966), 613—617. [613].
James Dickey "demands of the poet not the poem."

B145. Fields, Kenneth. "Strategies of Criticism," *Southern
Review*, N.S., II (Autumn 1966), 967—975. [968].
"Threatment of individuals is too brief."

B146. Rohr, Maria Rita. *Criticism*, VII (Fall 1965), 392.
James Dickey "capitalizes on his own verbal
brilliancy."

B147. "Soft Finger," *Times Literary Supplement*, October 29, 1964, p. 980.

> Dickey is never as "daring in specific verdicts as in abstract polemics."

B148. Spector, Robert D. "A Way to Say What A Man Can See," *Saturday Review*, IIL (February 13, 1965), 46 .

> Reviewer admires modern poetry more than Dickey does and finds Dickey's attitude alarming.

B149. Watson, Robert. "Two Books of Criticism," *Poetry*, CVII (February 1966), 332–333.

> Most criticisms are "too short to be effective; where he does take space to explain his position he can be very good."

B150. Willis, K. T. *Library Journal*, XC (February 1, 1965), 648.

> "This is a useful book...written by a seriously interested critic."

BABEL TO BYZANTIUM

B151. Adams, Phoebe. "Potpourri," *Atlantic Monthly*, CCXXI (May 1968), 114.

> James Dickey is lauded as "versatile, learned, and sympathetic."

B152. *American Literature*, XXXX (November 1968), 436.

> "For the most part the comments are amateurish chatter...."

B153. Brockman, Zoe. "Valuable Poetry Study," *Gastonia (N.C.) Gazette*, April 21, 1968, Sec. P, p. 4.
This book is "a must for both writers and students."

B154. Carroll, Paul. "James Dickey As Critic," *Chicago Review*, XX (November 1968), 82–87.
Reviewer defends Dickey from "The Hunting of the Dickey" sport among poets and lauds *Babel to Byzantium* as "Sanest, most invigorating and most fun to read since Randall Jarrell's *Poetry and the Age.*"

B155. *Choice*, V (October 1968), 950.
A short recommendation.

B156. Kaye, Howard. "Why Review Poetry," *New Republic,* CLVIII (June 29, 1968), 28–29.
The critic finds Dickey's attempt at "bodily experience" is "wrong about as often as it is right" and admits "I am about as far as possible from James Dickey's ideal reader...still he is an interesting man, and his book is...superior entertainment."

B157. Lask, Thomas. "Writer Turned Reader," *New York Times*, May 10, 1968, Sec. M, p. 45.
Critic predicts that this "is not a book that will be superseded because it deals with all that is fundamental, all that is 'necessary' and 'inevitable' in the writing and reading of poetry."

B158. Maloff, Saul. "Poet Takes His Turn as Critic,"

Washington Post, June 30, 1968, *Book Week*, p. 10. Praise for Dickey as "exact and felicitous" critic.

B159. Mills, Ralph J. Jr. "Brilliant Essays on Contemporary Poets," *Chicago Sun Times*, May 5, 1968, Book Week, p. 4.

Mills praises the book as a "brilliant and nearly complete critical chronicle of our poetry from the mid-1950's to the present."

B160. *Virginia Quarterly Review*, XXXXIV (Autumn 1968), cliii.

Dickey is seen as "critic of great promise."

LETTERS

B161. Brother Antoninus. *Sewanee Review*, LXIX (Spring 1961), 351–352.

Refers to A217; James Dickey's answer is A207.

B162. -- *Sewanee Review*, LXIX (Summer 1961), 511.

Another reference to A217; James Dickey's answer is A207.

B163. Hazel, Robert. "Or Would You Rather Be James Dickey," *Sewanee Review*, LXXII (Summer 1964), 551.

Refers to A226.

B164. Berry, Wendell. *Sewanee Review*, LXXII (Summer

1964), 552.
Refers to A226.

B165. Eaton, Charles. "Two Open Letters," *Sewanee Review*, LXXIII (Winter 1965), 176.
Refers to A226.

B166. "May Day Sermons Department," *Atlantic Monthly*, CCXIX (June 1967), 40–43.
Refers to A177.

B167. On "Robert Frost, Man or Myth," *Atlantic Monthly*, CCXIX (January 1967), 30.
Refers to A200.